Bible
Speaks
today

the message of

LAMENTATIONS

Series editors:
Alec Motyer (OT)
John Stott (NT)
Derek Tidball (Bible Themes)

All the royalties from this book have been irrevocably assigned to **Langham Literature**.

Langham Literature is one of the three programmes of **Langham Partnership**, founded by John Stott. Chris Wright is the International Ministries Director.

Langham Literature distributes evangelical books to pastors, theological students and seminary libraries in the Majority World, and fosters the writing and publishing of Christian literature in many regional languages. **Langham Preaching** establishes movements for biblical preaching in many countries, training people in how to study and preach the Bible in their own contexts, with continuous learning in local preachers' networks. **Langham Scholars** provides funding for gifted leaders to study for doctorates in Bible and Theology, and return to their home countries to teach future pastors in seminaries.

For further information, visit www.langham.org.

the message of

LAMENTATIONS

Honest to God
Revised edition

Christopher J. H. Wright

ivp
Academic
An imprint of InterVarsity Press
Downers Grove, Illinois

InterVarsity Press
P.O. Box 1400 | Downers Grove, IL 60515-1426
ivpress.com | email@ivpress.com

Inter-Varsity Press
Studio 101, The Record Hall, 16–16A Baldwins Gardens | London, EC1N 7RJ, UK
ivpbooks.com | ivp@ivpbooks.com

InterVarsity Press® is the publishing division of InterVarsity Christian Fellowship/USA®. For more information, visit intervarsity.org.

Inter-Varsity Press, England, originated within the Inter-Varsity Fellowship, now the Universities and Colleges Christian Fellowship, a student movement connecting Christian Unions in universities and colleges throughout Great Britain, and a member movement of the International Fellowship of Evangelical Students. That historic association is maintained, and all senior IVP staff and committee members subscribe to the UCCF Basis of Faith.

Unless otherwise stated, Scripture quotations are from the Holy Bible, New International Version (Anglicised edition). Copyright © 1979, 1984, 2011 by Biblica. Used by permission of Hodder & Stoughton, an Hachette company. All rights reserved. 'NIV' is a registered trademark of Biblica, UK trademark number 1448790.

This edition published 2023.

Cover design: Cindy Kiple
Images: © MarkSkalny / iStock / Getty Images Plus

USA ISBN 978-1-5140-0639-9 (print) | USA ISBN 978-1-5140-0640-5 (digital)
UK ISBN 978-1-78974-441-5 (print) | UK ISBN 978-1-78359-620-1 (digital)

Typeset in Great Britain by CRB Associates, Potterhanworth, Lincolnshire

Printed in the United States of America ♾

Library of Congress Cataloging-in-Publication Data
A catalog record for this book is available from the Library of Congress.

British Library Cataloguing-in-Publication Data
A catalogue record for this book is available from the British Library.

31 30 29 28 27 26 25 24 23 | 11 10 9 8 7 6 5 4 3 2 1

To
Syria's children

Cry of a Pakistani woman during the floods of 2011 by Gill Phillips.

Contents

Bible Speaks today

GENERAL PREFACE

The Bible Speaks Today describes three series of expositions, based on the books of the Old and New Testaments, and on Bible themes that run through the whole of Scripture. Each series is characterized by a threefold ideal:

- to expound the biblical text with accuracy
- to relate it to contemporary life, and
- to be readable.

These books are, therefore, not 'commentaries', for the commentary seeks rather to elucidate the text than to apply it, and tends to be a work rather of reference than of literature. Nor, on the other hand, do they contain the kinds of 'sermons' that attempt to be contemporary and readable without taking Scripture seriously enough. The contributors to The Bible Speaks Today series are all united in their convictions that God still speaks through what he has spoken, and that nothing is more necessary for the life, health and growth of Christians than that they should hear what the Spirit is saying to them through his ancient – yet ever modern – Word.

ALEC MOTYER
JOHN STOTT
DEREK TIDBALL
Series editors

Author's preface

Who am I, Lord? I have often pondered in these past months. Who am I to be writing a commentary on Lamentations, as a man of few sorrows and very little acquainted with grief – few and little, at any rate (for none of us is immune to life's sorrows), in comparison with the scale of devastating loss and unspeakable suffering that is memorialized in this book? How can such tear-soaked words be truly heard, how can the scenes they portray even be imagined, let alone commented on? Mere exposition of the searing, sobbing, stinging lines seemed at times intrusive – like the TV commentators who have to add their redundant words to the all-too-glaring agonies of those whose lives and families are torn to pieces in the world's worst destructions of war or nature. For that is the kind of world Lamentations hurls us into.

But alongside that question, a more remorseful one. Why had I neglected this book for so long and never really studied it in depth before? And in that respect, of course, I confess to the same neglect of Lamentations that seems sadly typical of most Christian people and churches. Since we seem to have lost the willingness, the vocabulary, or even the capacity, to engage in authentic biblical lament (at least in public worship and certainly in the West), what use have we for a book with such a name? We hardly know how to use the numerous *psalms* of lament, let alone a whole book full of (almost but not quite) unrelieved grief and protest. Ironically, by giving no attention to the book of Lamentations, we join those within the book itself who passed by Lady Zion, shaking their heads but offering no comfort to the desolate suffering city and people. Perhaps, then, writing this commentary has been something of an apology to one so long neglected. Again and again Lady Zion, now a weeping widow, asks God, her neighbours and us the readers of the book simply to 'Look and see . . .' To write a commentary on her words is to respond to her pleading voice – however belatedly – and to invite others to do the same.

Resources for the study of the book are satisfyingly plentiful. The bibliography lists those I found most useful, along with some that I was not able to consult but that are frequently referenced elsewhere. Paul House combines very detailed attention to all the critical dimensions and dilemmas in the text with sensitivity to the theological and pastoral issues raised by the book. Adele Berlin and Kathleen O'Connor are representative of those who feel the tone of the book is predominantly accusatory of God himself, leaving us with an unanswered question – a counter-testimony to the traditional and deep-rooted faith of Israel in the goodness and faithfulness of their God. While not following them to such conclusions, I find their commentaries deeply sensitive to the poignancy and poetry of the text, and (especially in O'Connor's case) to both personal suffering and the screaming injustices of our world. Daniel Berrigan wrote his reflections on the book (it is hardly a commentary in the standard sense) in the immediate aftermath of 9/11 and the subsequent bombing of Afghanistan. His powerful juxtaposition of the horrors of the text with the horrors of today is both prophetic and profoundly poetic in its own way. Robin Parry seemed to me the most sure-footed guide, with exceptionally clear exegesis of the most disputed sections of the text, along with a wide-ranging and richly stimulating series of theological reflections that probe not only the resonances of the book within a Christian canonical reading, but also the contemporary relevance of the book in the realm of international politics and conflicts.

The painting *Cry* was inspired by an image of a mother lamenting the suffering of her children in the midst of extreme floods in Northern Pakistan in 2011. The artist Gill Phillips was particularly moved by the dignity and silent cry of the woman. It seems an appropriate image for Lady Zion and her lost children in Lamentations.

The suffering of the children in the siege of Jerusalem is one of the marked features of the book. It seems the author can never get them out of his mind – along with their distraught and starving mothers. As then, so today. Representatives of children's agencies have said that 2014 was the worst year ever for the world's children. Untold millions of little lives have been destroyed – by abduction, industrial and domestic slavery, sex trafficking, rape and abuse, mutilation, conscription into child armies, the horrendous toll of death, crippling injury, orphanhood and trauma in war zones, and now even the deliberate targeting of children as victims of revenge – all of which is the cost of the diabolical bloodlust of adult humanity in their conflicts all over the globe. Such child suffering is simply incalculable, and surely it breaks the heart of God, whose own birth into a world of violent oppression meant a refugee's flight for Jesus and the murder of innocent infants in Bethlehem for the paranoid rage of a petty tyrant. Syria's children, to whom this book is dedicated and with whom we have some personal connection through loving friends in the region, represent the suffering children of the world. Lord, have mercy.

I finished the book in Advent and write this preface in the season of Epiphany – reminders that the Lord who appeared once in humility, to bear in the person of his own Son the sin and suffering of the world, will return to bring an end to all sin and suffering, all crying and tears, all death and destruction. And we are among those who long for his appearing. For, as Psalm 96 exults to anticipate, the whole creation will rejoice when God comes to judge the earth and put all things right. Lamentations is a powerful and essential voice which we must hear. It is an integral canonical word within that 'God-breathed and profitable' scripture through which 'the Bible speaks today'. But thanks be to God that, in the context of the Bible's whole story, with its gospel centre and new creation climax, it is not the last word.

CHRIS WRIGHT
Epiphany 2015

Chief abbreviations

Select bibliography

In the notes, commentaries are referred to by author's surname only. Other works listed below are referred to by author name and short title.

Commentaries

Berlin, A., *Lamentations: A Commentary*, Old Testament Library (Louisville: Westminster John Knox, 2002).

Berrigan, D., *Lamentations: From New York to Kabul and Beyond* (Lanham: Sheed and Ward, 2002).

Coulibaly, I., 'Lamentations', in T. Adeyemo (ed.), *Africa Bible Commentary* (Grand Rapids: Zondervan, 2010), pp. 951–958.

Dearman, J. A., *Jeremiah and Lamentations*, The NIV Application Commentary (Grand Rapids: Zondervan, 2002).

Harrison, R. K., *Jeremiah and Lamentations*, Tyndale Old Testament Commentaries (Leicester and Downers Grove: IVP, 1973).

Hillers, D. R., *Lamentations*, Anchor Yale Bible (2nd edn, New Haven: Yale University Press, 2009).

House, P. R., *Lamentations*, Word Biblical Commentary 23B (Nashville: Thomas Nelson, 2004).

Lalleman, H., *Jeremiah and Lamentations*, Tyndale Old Testament Commentaries (Leicester and Downers Grove: IVP, 2013).

Longman III, T., *Jeremiah, Lamentations*, New International Biblical Commentary (Peabody: Hendrickson; Milton Keynes: Paternoster, 2008).

O'Connor, K., *Lamentations and the Tears of the World* (Maryknoll: Orbis, 2002).

Parry, R., *Lamentations*, Two Horizons Old Testament Commentary (Grand Rapids: Eerdmans, 2010).

Provan, I., *Lamentations*, New Century Bible Commentary (Grand Rapids: Eerdmans, 1991).

Re'emi, S. P., *A Commentary on the Book of Lamentations: God's People in Crisis*, International Theological Commentary (Grand Rapids: Eerdmans; Edinburgh: Handsel, 1984).

The following are commentaries I was not able to consult, but which are often referenced in several of those above.

Dobbs-Allsopp, F. W., *Lamentations*, Interpretation (Louisville: Westminster John Knox, 2002).

Renkema, J., *Lamentations*, Historical Commentary on the Old Testament (Leuven: Peeters, 1998).

Westermann, C., *Lamentations: Issues and Interpretation* (Edinburgh: T. & T. Clark, 1994).

Other works

Parry, R., 'Lamentations and the Poetic Politics of Prayer', *Tyndale Bulletin* 62.1 (2011), pp. 65–88.

Parry, R., and H. A. Thomas (eds.), *Great Is Thy Faithfulness? Reading Lamentations as Sacred Scripture* (Eugene: Pickwick, 2011).

Slavitt, D. R., *The Book of Lamentations: A Meditation and Translation* (Baltimore: Johns Hopkins, 2001).

Thomas, H., *'Until He Looks Down and Sees': The Message and Meaning of the Book of Lamentations* (Cambridge: Grove Books, 2009).

Webb, B. G., *Five Festal Garments: Christian Reflections on the Song of Songs, Ruth, Lamentations, Ecclesiastes and Esther* (Leicester: Apollos; Downers Grove: IVP, 2000).

Williams, A., 'Biblical Lament and Political Protest', *Cambridge Papers* 23.1 (Cambridge: Jubilee Centre, 2014).

Introduction

Lamentations is a book for today.

In a world where the tide of human suffering threatens to overwhelm whatever dykes we put in place to contain it, is there any book of the Bible more relevant than this book that gives voice to the most awful pain imaginable? And yet is there any book of the Bible more neglected? Christian churches seem to have forgotten it is there at all, so rarely is it ever read or preached.[1] The only connection many Christians (of a certain age) might have to the book is when they sing Thomas Chisholm's hymn 'Great Is Thy Faithfulness', and even then they might not be aware that some of its lines are drawn from Lamentations 3:23.

It is a grievous loss, this neglect of Lamentations, for three reasons. First, it disrespects the voice of those whose suffering the book so poignantly commemorates. It stifles an appeal to be heard that addresses us from the generation that endured the siege and destruction of Jerusalem in 588–587 BC and the slaughter and captivity that followed. To ignore that voice is like throwing a drape over all the war memorials that commemorate the names of those who died in wartime, and all that was suffered by their families at that time. Part of the horror of human suffering is to be unheard, forgotten and nameless, thrown aside with all the long-lost detritus of aeons of human brutality.[2] Lamentations is a *summons to remember* realities endured by real people like ourselves, to bear witness and pay heed to their voice.

---

[1] Not so in Jewish communities, where the book is still read annually on Tisha b'Av, the ninth day of the month of Av, occurring in July or August, as a way of commemorating the suffering of Jews in the original destruction of Jerusalem by the Babylonians in 587 BC, in its destruction by the Romans in AD 70, and in later pogroms against Jews, culminating in the Holocaust.

[2] That is why commemoration of wartime suffering includes many national monuments to 'the Unknown Soldier'.

Second, such neglect deprives the contemporary church of the language of lament – a whole genre and vocabulary given to us by God in his word for a reason. Lament, of course, is not confined to the book of Lamentations. There are many psalms of lament (the largest single category of psalms in the book, which is remarkable in itself, given that the Hebrew title of that book is 'The Praises'). We find raw lament poured out by Jeremiah and by Job in their struggles with God and humanity. We find lament on the lips of Jesus on the cross, articulating his intense suffering in the opening words of Psalm 22.

But when did you last hear biblical lament on the lips of Christians in a service of worship? Perhaps that question betrays its location in the relative comfort of the Western church, for the abundant and powerful language of lament is certainly to be found on the lips of believers in parts of the world where their suffering has been intense and seemingly interminable, from African slaves to Syrian refugees. They know what it is to be hunted to death by fierce enemies, to suffer loss of land, homes, families, lives and livelihoods. They know what it is to cry out to God in pain, protest and appeal. Lamentations speaks to them and for them.[3] But when we live in a global village and are more aware of the tears of the world than ever before, are we not *all* called to weep with those who weep by sharing their voice in the God-given language of lament? Or will we be among the passers-by who look and see but have no comfort to offer (1:12, 16–17)?

Third, never to read Lamentations is to miss the challenge and reward of wrestling with the massive theological issues that permeate its poetry. How can the ultimate extremes of suffering be endured alongside faith in the living God whom we have learned from the Scriptures and in experience to be all-loving and good? Even if the events causing suffering in this instance are recognized and accepted as the outcome of God's anger and judgment, after centuries of warning and pleading by God through Moses and the prophets, has not the savage flood of implacable evil and brutality on the part of those human enemies whom God has used as agents of his judgment, gone beyond all bounds? And if anarchy, death and destruction stalk the land, can the centre hold[4] – the centre of Israel's faith in YHWH

---

[3] This is not to suggest that those suffering in today's world do so under the judgment of God, in the way that Lamentations repeatedly acknowledges as the case for Judah in 587 BC.

[4] The allusion is to lines from W. B. Yeats's famous poem in the wake of the First World War, 'The Second Coming': 'Things fall apart; the centre cannot hold; / Mere anarchy is loosed upon the world.'

the covenant God of faithfulness and mercy? Yes it can, and yes it does – right in the structural centre of the book (3:21–24). But that affirmation of hope is surrounded on both sides with an unremitting litany of unresolved suffering, from the opening to the closing verses of the book. We are thereby forced to cast our doctrine of the character of God into the furnace of dire experience in this fallen world, and find it again as refined gold. For as Christian readers of this text we cannot isolate it from the revelation of the rest of Scripture – where we find that God cast himself into that furnace in the person of his Son, Jesus Christ. And in Lamentations we will hear a voice like his, speaking as he might have done from the cross, plumbing the depths of suffering but trusting in the faithfulness of God.

But before we reflect on such theological challenges, we need to see the book in its own context.

1. Lamentations in its own world

a. The event

The circumstances that gave rise to this remarkable book of five intense poems were almost certainly[5] the events surrounding the destruction of Jerusalem by the Babylonians under Nebuchadnezzar in 587 BC. Though Judah and Jerusalem suffered other invasions and attacks during the long monarchy period, nothing on a lesser scale than the total devastation of 587 BC would seem consistent with the sheer magnitude of what is described, especially in chapters 2 and 4. So what did happen?

Babylon had risen to power after the collapse of the Assyrian Empire. In 609 BC, Josiah, the last good king of Judah and its most ardent (but ultimately unsuccessful) reformer, was killed in the battle of Megiddo, trying to prevent the Egyptians from coming to the aid of Assyria. For a very short time, Judah came under Egypt's power and they put Jehoiakim on the throne of Jerusalem. The rising power of Babylon, however, was unstoppable. Under their new young king Nebuchadnezzar they expanded north and west. In 605 BC, Nebuchadnezzar routed the Egyptians at the decisive battle of Carchemish, and from that date on Babylon was the unassailable imperial power in the whole region for the next seventy years.

---

[5] Some scholars regard the date of the book as indeterminate – perhaps composed much later in the exile, even if the event described in the book was the fall of Jerusalem. See e.g. Provan, pp. 11–15.

From that date also, 605 BC, the political future of Judah hung on what stance they would take towards the great power – submission or rebellion. Throughout this whole period, Jeremiah repeatedly warned the people of Judah and the political leaders in Jerusalem that the combination of their unrepented sins of social oppression and rampant idolatry with their political folly in seeking unstable alliances against Babylon would ultimately bring upon them the judgment of God mediated through the agency of Babylon itself – and it would be terrifyingly destructive when it came. But they would not listen, branded him a traitor, and tried to silence him with violence and imprisonment. Indeed, in that same year, 605 BC, King Jehoiakim deliberately burnt the whole scroll containing twenty-three years of Jeremiah's preaching – a breathtaking act of blatant defiance of the word of God.

In 597 Jehoiakim chose to rebel against Babylon. Nebuchadnezzar quickly launched a retributive attack. Jehoiakim conveniently died (or was murdered), and his son Jehoiachin, with greater wisdom, surrendered the city. That act spared the city the worst of Nebuchadnezzar's wrath – temporarily; but a portion of the leading citizens were taken off to Babylon in the First Deportation, among them a young man called Ezekiel. Nebuchadnezzar then appointed Zedekiah, another son of Josiah, to the throne in Jerusalem, expecting him to behave as conquered vassal states should – with obedient submission and tribute.

For ten years King Zedekiah vacillated, seemingly swayed to and fro by conflicting factions in the political leadership in Jerusalem, and unwilling to heed the advice of Jeremiah that the least destructive course of action would be to submit to Babylon's authority. Yet again, he led Judah into rebellion against Babylon. This time Nebuchadnezzar decided to finish the job. He invaded Judah and destroyed its towns and villages.[6] Then he besieged Jerusalem. The account can be read in Jeremiah 52 – bald and factual, but with enough detail for our imagination to picture the horror of it all. The siege lasted for eighteen months, during which all the worst effects of siege warfare ensued – the ending of food supplies, starvation, death and disease. Finally, in 587 BC the Babylonians broke through Jerusalem's wall and invaded the city. The army fled at night, taking King

---

[6] Archaeological evidence suggests that about 80% of the towns and villages of Judah that existed in the late seventh century were destroyed or abandoned during the sixth-century Babylonian invasion and its aftermath. The destruction of Judah was massive. See Parry, 'Lamentations and the Poetic Politics of Prayer', pp. 65–88.

Zedekiah with them, but they were caught and scattered. The king was captured and taken to Nebuchadnezzar, who delivered him to the fate of rebel vassals. His sons were killed in front of him. Then he was blinded and carried off in chains to die in Babylon. Meanwhile, those of the people who had survived the starvation and the slaughter were marched off on a thousand-mile journey by foot into exile in far-off Babylon, leaving only a few poor survivors behind in the stricken land of Judah – Jeremiah among them. (And even that fragile fragment of the nation eventually took flight out of the land, seeking refuge in Egypt, taking Jeremiah with them, against his advice and his will.) The city of Jerusalem itself was then systematically destroyed, its palaces and houses burnt and its walls razed to the ground. Worst of all, the temple of YHWH, built by Solomon four hundred years earlier, was defiled, looted and then burnt. Nothing remained of the city and the nation and the house that all bore God's name. Nothing but smouldering ruins and rubble, death and dust – except for a small exiled community in Babylon, among whom were Ezekiel and Daniel, and from whom God would eventually rebuild his people and restore them for his mission and theirs among the nations. But that day was a long way off, and scarcely a glimmer of it pricks the dark horizon of Lamentations.

This was unquestionably the most traumatic moment in the whole history of the Old Testament. Not only was there massive human suffering at every level of physical and emotional experience, not only the devastating demolition and incineration of their ancient and beautiful city, but there was also the utter humiliation of their national pride as a small but independent nation that had a history in the land stretching back to Joshua. And along with that went the devastating undermining of all that they had thought was theologically guaranteed – the Davidic monarchy, the city of Zion, and the very temple of their omnipotent God (or was he?). All gone. What possible future could there be? And how could the present even be endured? It is out of that unspeakable pain that Lamentations speaks, daring to describe the indescribable and to utter the unutterable – and to do so in poetry of astonishing beauty and intricacy, though soaked in tears.

b. The Poet

So who is the author? Whose voice speaks in these pain-filled poems? The plain answer is that we do not know, since the book is anonymous, without any name claimed by the author or inserted by an editor in the Hebrew text. 'The Lamentations of Jeremiah', says the book's title in the KJV, reflecting a traditional ascription that goes back a very long way. The Septuagint Greek translation (from the late second century BC) has these words in its opening verse: 'And it came to pass after Israel had gone into captivity, and Jerusalem was laid waste, that Jeremiah sat weeping and composed this lament over Jerusalem and said . . .' Similar wording, ascribing the book to Jeremiah, is found in the Syriac, in the Targum (early Jewish commentary in Aramaic) and in the Vulgate (Latin). This would be the reason why the Septuagint places Lamentations immediately after the book of Jeremiah, an order that has been followed in Christian Bibles ever since. It fits very neatly there, after we have read about the destruction of Jerusalem in Jeremiah 52 and before we head off to join Ezekiel among the exiles in Babylon.

However, in the Hebrew canon, Lamentations is included among the third section of the canon, the Writings, as one of the five *Megilloth* (scrolls; the others being Ruth, Esther, Song of Solomon and Ecclesiastes). This probably does not mean that the Hebrew tradition regarded the book as *not* coming from Jeremiah, but simply that it was among the texts used liturgically on certain commemorative days. Lamentations is read on Tisha b'Av – the ninth day of the month of Av (in July or August) – to remember the destruction of Jerusalem and the temple in 587 BC, again in AD 70, and the many terrible times of persecution of Jewish people culminating in the Holocaust.

The view that Jeremiah was the author of Lamentations held its place in Christian and Jewish tradition until it began to be challenged from the eighteenth century by Western scholars. Today, the majority of scholars reckon that Jeremiah was probably not the author, though the reasons given for this are not always entirely convincing.

- Some point to what they see as many differences of style and language from what we find in the book of Jeremiah. However, there are some strong similarities too, and arguments from literary style (especially in a book as small as Lamentations) are often rather subjective.
- It is thought that the attribution to Jeremiah may be connected with the note in 2 Chronicles 35:25 telling us that Jeremiah wrote laments for the death in battle of King Josiah, but since that was

clearly a different historical event from the destruction of Jerusalem in 587 BC, it proves nothing about his authorship of the book of Lamentations. Very true. But it does indicate that Jeremiah could compose laments, something we could have guessed from the powerful poetry of grief in his own book.

- It is said that Jeremiah, with his sustained critique of the kings of Judah after Josiah, would not have spoken of Zedekiah in the words of Lamentations 4:20 as 'the LORD's anointed, our very life breath', or expressed the hope of living 'under his shadow'. It is true, of course, that there was little love lost between the prophet and the king in those terrible final ten years, but Jeremiah would not have questioned the de facto anointing of Zedekiah as the legitimate Davidic king of Judah and the role he was supposed to play in protecting his people. He simply disagreed (radically) with the policy and actions (or rather, the lack of them) that Zedekiah adopted in his vacillating political stance, caught between feuding factions in his own government circles. Lamentations 4:20 articulates the forlorn hope of the people ('we'), which the poet (or Jeremiah himself) could easily have expressed (speaking as their personified identity) without believing it would be fulfilled.

- In the same chapter, it is argued that Jeremiah would never have joined in the vain longing for help from another nation (probably Egypt) that is referred to in 4:17. But we should remember that the poet of Lamentations 4 is the personified voice of the people, speaking out their thoughts and feelings in the midst of the siege. So it is not impossible that he would have voiced their sin and folly and false hopes without necessarily sharing them. Daniel and Nehemiah formulate prayers that combine lament and confession, though neither of them were personally guilty of the sins they mention.[7] Jeremiah did the same (e.g. Jer. 14:7, 19–22).

- The writer of Lamentations 4 (indeed of the whole book) seems to have been an eyewitness of the events described – so graphically are they portrayed, and with such personal impact. In 4:20, he speaks of the capture of King Zedekiah after his escape from Jerusalem. Jeremiah could not have witnessed that himself, of course, since he was imprisoned in the courtyard of the military

---

7 In their great prayers of intercession in Dan. 9 and Neh. 9.

7

citadel in the city right to the end of the siege and was eventually released by the Babylonians. But even if the writer did not *see* the capture of the king, the news of it would have very quickly reached every last survivor in the city, including Jeremiah. The Babylonians would have made sure of that.

So in my own opinion, there is nothing in the book that *could not* have been written by Jeremiah. And there is much in the book that certainly *sounds* like Jeremiah, or has been made to sound like him. But that, of course, is not to claim that it *was* written by Jeremiah. Perhaps the strongest argument against Jeremiah's authorship (since it has theological and textual substance) is the question whether the Jeremiah who had already received the words of incredible hope and assurance contained in the Book of Consolation (Jer. 30 – 33), who had invested his last seventeen shekels to buy a field as a pointer to a future when people would farm the land again (Jer. 32), who had already written a letter to the first group of exiles that contained the wonderful promise of Jeremiah 29:10–11 – whether that Jeremiah would have sunk to such depths of questioning despair in this book. Would he not have had more to say than the brief shafts of hope in the middle of chapter 3? Probably he could have. But we should not underestimate the severity of the trauma caused by the events of 588–587 BC – even for one who had foreseen and foretold them and had seen beyond them to a future restoration. Living right through the barbarity, brutality and burning, having witnessed it close up, and seeing the continuing unbearable suffering of his own people in the aftermath, even a prophet of ultimate hope was not going to sing 'Look on the bright side of life' with the cold comfort of 'It will all turn out fine in the end'. For the blunt fact was that for that whole generation, it would not. It was not the end for Israel and God's ultimate purpose through them, but it *was* the end for those doomed to die in the conflagration of Jerusalem or in exile thereafter. Their suffering was terrible and terminal. And Lamentations goes there with them. It is not inconceivable that Jeremiah shared the darkness of that pit, or at least gave voice to it on their behalf.

In the end we have to come back to where we started: whoever wrote this book has chosen not to disclose his name and we need to respect that fact, treating it as possibly intentional. For that reason, I have chosen to refer to the author simply as 'the Poet'. And I do so throughout the book, except in chapter 3, where the Poet describes himself as 'the Man', assuming, as I do, that there is a unity of identity of the implied main speaker in each chapter. In my opinion, the view that Lamentations consists of a miscellany of laments by different authors over an indeterminate time span is very convincingly and decisively outweighed by the view that the book is an intricate composition by a single mind, working out a profound and battle-scarred theology in the midst of appalling suffering, yet doing so in poetry of remarkable verbal power, dramatic dialogue and structural skill.

c. The poetry

It is well known that great art, great music and great literature can emerge out of great pain. This does not lessen the reality of the suffering of the artist, composer or writer, but it points to something creative and redemptive in the human person, made in the image of God, which can bring forth a thing of beauty in the midst of surrounding ugliness, brutality and evil. Nowhere is this more true than in the book of Lamentations. As we have said above, the suffering out of which it emerged was incalculably great. The Poet himself could find no adequate comparison for it. 'Your wound is as deep as the sea,' he says to Lady Zion (2:13) – boundlessly, immeasurably deep as the ocean. Yet in talking about it, talking to her, addressing the readers, turning to God, confessing, lamenting, accusing, trusting, hoping – he produces poetry of amazing density and intensity, opening up vistas of imagination in three or four pregnant Hebrew words at a time, line by pulsing line. He portrays the horror of what he had witnessed sometimes in language that is agonizingly literal, and sometimes in a turmoil of metaphors that tumble over one another in a destructive avalanche. There are several formal features of the poetry of Lamentations that we can mention, since it is important to understand them, even without knowledge of the original Hebrew.

i. Acrostic

'Acrostic' means alphabetical. Hebrew poets seemed to like this method of arranging a poem, in which verses begin with successive letters of the Hebrew alphabet (of which there are twenty-two). Psalms 111 and 112 are matching acrostics – one about the Lord, the second about the person who fears the Lord. The most spectacular example is Psalm 119, where the author has produced twenty-two stanzas in which all eight lines of each stanza begin with the same Hebrew letter (as most English Bibles show).

In Lamentations, chapters 1–4 are all acrostic. Chapter 5 drops the acrostic sequence of opening letters, but still has twenty-two verses, preserving the external form of the previous chapters. We cannot know exactly what the author's intention was in choosing this form, but we can recognize several effects on the reader (and possibly on the Poet himself and those for whom he spoke). First, it keeps us moving on inexorably, unable to pause for too long on any of the scenes, until we come back to read it through once more. There is a drive and rhythm. This is a *journey* through grief, not wallowing in it. Second, there is a sense of intentional completeness. It is as if the Poet says, 'Here is all our pain, from A to Z.' It is an encyclopaedia of suffering. Nothing more can be said, or needs to be. Third, though, it brings some control to the chaotic swirl that deep trauma and grief produce. Such times send us into a spin, an unending vicious cycle of emotions. The alphabetic sequence calls for ordered thought, and that becomes theologically and spiritually productive in chapter 3 and prayerfully, cautiously hopeful in chapter 5.

It is almost impossible to capture this acrostic effect in English translation and no Bible (that I know of) attempts it. However, some commentators have tried. Here are some extracts from David Slavitt's translation, using alphabetic sequencing:

> All the gold has been dulled, its pure luster lost. And the precious gems are strewn stones in the streets.

> Bright sons of Zion, worth their weight in gold and diamonds, are scattered too, like shards from a broken pot.

> Cruel jackals are tender and give suck to their young. More cruel is the daughter of my people, who cares for her children less than an ostrich in the wild.

> Dirty, hungry, thirsty, children complain and beg, but no one comes to their aid.

> Everywhere ruin attends . . .
> (4:1–5)[8]

---

[8] Slavitt, *Lamentations*, p. 79.

In chapter 3, the acrostic effect is tripled, as all three lines in each stanza begin with the same successive letter. Here is Slavitt's translation:

Afflicted am I and beset, a man whom God in his wrath has abased.
Abused by his rod and broken, I am driven into the darkness.
Against me, he turned his hand, and again and again.

Bones broken, wasted, I am besieged and battered.
Bitterness is my portion and tribulation.
Banished, I dwell in the darkest darkness like those long dead.

Chained so I cannot escape and walled in, I am a captive.
Crying for help, I call out, but he will not hear my prayer.
Crooked are all my paths, which he has blocked with boulders.

Desolate am I and desperate . . .
(3:1–10)

ii. Qinah metre

The poems share features of both *dirges* (that is, funeral songs for the dead, or in response to some terrible calamity) and *laments* (that is, songs that appeal to God in the midst of suffering, persecution or inexplicable violence, with a sense of protest and sometimes with hope and renewed praise). And often such poems use a metre known as *qinah*. Whereas most Hebrew poetry (in the Psalms or poetic sections of the prophets) used a form of metre that tends to balance out the number of stressed syllables in both halves of the lines of poetry (often 3 + 3), the *qinah* metre shortens the second half, so that it is typically 3 + 2 stresses. This creates a kind of limping or moaning effect, which matches the mood of such poetry. This metre is used predominantly throughout Lamentations (though not rigidly in every verse).

It is very hard to capture the effect of such a metre in English – particularly since English (like many other modern languages) usually requires more words to express what two or three words of condensed Hebrew poetry can convey. Delbert Hillers attempts to make this feature visible and audible in some of his translation. For example:

How deserted lies the city – that was once full of people!
    The greatest among nations – is now like a widow;

> The noblest of states – is set to forced labour
> By night she weeps aloud – tears on her cheeks.
> There is no one to comfort her – of all her lovers
> . . .
> All her gates are desolate. – Her priests sigh.
> Her young women are troubled, – and she is bitter.
> Her enemies now are supreme – her foes, at ease.
> . . .
> Her children were driven as prisoners – before the enemy
> And there has departed from Zion – all her splendour.
>
> (1:1–6)[9]

iii. Dialogue and characters

The Poet heightens the dramatic tension of his portrayal of Jerusalem's suffering by speaking through different 'characters' whose voices interact with one another – especially in chapters 1–2. Some scholars distinguish several different voices in chapters 3, 4 and 5 from the two that are clearly identified in chapters 1 and 2. But it seems to bring greater clarity and coherence if we see continuity between the narrator of chapters 1–2, the Man who announces himself so forcefully at the start of chapter 3, the voice of continuing grief in chapter 4, and finally the voice that leads the people in a prayer of combined lament, confession and appeal in chapter 5.

Continuity of identity, however, does not mean sameness of content or mood. The Poet himself seems to move from somewhat objective observation with theological comment in chapter 1, to utter shock at the total devastation in the city, and overwhelming grief and sympathy for its women and children, in chapter 2. In chapter 3 he identifies himself totally with the suffering of the city in a passionate outburst at what God has done to it (him), but then finds a degree of hope and calm in the midst of the storm. It is a fragile hope, though, and the prolonged suffering of his people continues to absorb his grief through chapter 4, till he turns it into community prayer in chapter 5.

The Poet introduces the two major characters in the book at the start: himself (as the narrator, or dialogue partner), and the city of Jerusalem personified as a woman (a widow who had once been a queen, 1:1). This

---

[9] Hillers, p. 61.

'city-woman' (as we shall sometimes call her) is named in 1:6 as 'daughter of Zion' (ESV). The phrase expresses identity (that is, it means 'Daughter Zion', as in the 2011 NIV, not 'Zion's daughter'). It is a term of respect or affection ('Dear Zion' is Adele Berlin's rendering). We shall call her Lady Zion.

So the Poet begins by describing what has happened to Lady Zion, until suddenly she interrupts with a brief appeal of her own (1:9c). When he has finished (for the moment), she takes over, pleading with God and passers-by to see her suffering (1:12–22), interrupted briefly by the Poet (1:17).

In chapter 2, the Poet describes what has happened to the city, until he can say no more for weeping (2:1–11). Then he turns to Lady Zion, seeking (in vain) to comfort her, and urging her to cry out to God – for her children if not for herself (2:13–19). She responds, but only with words that question and challenge God (2:20–22).

The dialogue in chapters 1–2 sets up what seems an unresolvable tension. The Poet is shocked and horrified. Lady Zion is desolate, shamed, comfortless, and yet somehow finds enough voice to plead, question – and even demand. After the end of chapter 2 Lady Zion never speaks again, but remains onstage as a silent witness. The Poet takes upon himself the identity of Jerusalem in chapter 3, and engages in dialogue with himself (3:16–24), with the people (3:40), but mostly with God (3:43–66). In chapter 4 the Poet speaks descriptively of the suffering of 'my people' (4:6), and they sometimes speak for themselves (4:17–20). A prophetic voice interrupts at the end with an oracle about Edom and one of hope for Lady Zion (4:21–22). Finally, in chapter 5, the Poet leads the people in a corporate prayer in which only their voice is heard.

In addition to those who actually speak in the poems, there is a cast of other players on the stage, whose voices we hear only indirectly if at all. There are the lovers and friends who had betrayed Lady Zion (1:2, 19). There are the enemies who mock and taunt even as they rape and pillage (1:7, 10, 21; 2:16). There are the passers-by who either say nothing to comfort Lady Zion (1:12), or express only astonishment (2:15). There are the princes, priests, prophets and elders, all of whom have failed to prevent the disaster and now suffer in it along with the poorest slaves (1:19; 2:9–10, 14; 4:5, 7–8, 13; 5:12–14). There are the strapping young men and soldiers who have been trampled on, and the young girls who have been raped and humiliated in the dust (1:15; 2:10, 21; 5:11). And above all, there are the mothers and the children, whose cries as they die of starvation, with a fate worse than death beyond that, move the Poet again and again (1:11; 2:11–12, 19, 20; 4:3–4, 10). Lamentations is like a great living canvas in which our eyes are drawn to one character or group after another at every level of society in their voiced or voiceless suffering, till the whole scene is as densely packed with people as the poetry is with words.

There is one voice we never hear. God does not speak in the whole book of Lamentations.[10] Heaven is silent. Which does not necessarily mean that heaven is deaf or blind. We shall consider later what Kathleen O'Connor calls 'the power of the missing voice'.

iv. Structure

One last feature of the poetic artistry of the book needs a mention – its interesting structure. The book has five chapters, which suggests that chapter 3 might be the central focus of the message of the book as a whole. That impression is strengthened by the intensification of the acrostic pattern in that chapter. In chapters 1 and 2, the Poet writes twenty-two stanzas of three lines each, in which the first line of each stanza starts with the letters of the alphabet in sequence. However, in chapter 3, he triples the acrostic intensity by starting all three lines of each of the twenty-two stanzas with the same letter (like AAA, BBB, CCC, etc.). Our Bibles turn each line of chapter 3 into a separate verse, and for that reason it has sixty-six one-line verses, even though it is actually the same length as chapters 1 and 2 with their twenty-two three-line verses.

Further strengthening the centrality of chapter 3 is the fact that right at the centre of that chapter – that is, at the apparent centre of the book as a whole – come the strongest words of positive hope and theological affirmation that the book can muster (3:31–33, preceded, of course, by the famous lines of 3:22–24).

And yet, and yet – it is not quite the perfect centre, for the Poet has so structured chapters 4 and 5 that they bring the book to a waning, limping end, rather like the *qinah* metre that dominates the poetry itself. Chapter 4 is acrostic, but has two-line stanzas, while chapter 5 has twenty-two one-line-only verses. As a result, chapters 4 and 5 together are the same

---

[10] Except for the reported words of God in 3:57, but these had been spoken to the Poet during some previous experience, not directly into the situation portrayed in Lamentations itself. It is also possible that 4:21–22 is intended as a prophetic word from God, shining a brief ray of hope into the darkness.

length as chapter 3. This gradual shortening of the chapters and stanzas makes the book slowly ebb away, like the lives of those who suffer in its pages.

It is as if the Poet has stated his central theological conviction (in the heart of chapter 3), but cannot for that reason simply ignore or dismiss the terrible reality of continuing suffering that his people are enduring. The pain isn't over yet, just because hope has spoken a brief word. Hope is thus theologically centred in the Poet's faith, but structurally decentred in the Poet's experienced reality. The truth about God's ultimate faithfulness and compassion does not erase that pain or silence the questions it generates. They continue in the unresolved present and into an as yet unknown future, even as the book ends.

2. Lamentations and suffering

'Lamentations? I don't think I've ever really read it,' said a friend (though she had half a century of personal Christian faith) on hearing about my work on this commentary. 'I sometimes wonder why it's in the Bible at all.' Why indeed. I was pondering that very question when I heard Richard Flanagan interviewed on BBC Radio 4 after winning the 2014 Man Booker Prize for his book *The Narrow Road to the Deep North*.[11] The book is fiction, but based on the suffering of his own father on the infamous Thailand–Burma railway as a prisoner of the Japanese in the Second World War. Flanagan said that his father had never harboured hatred for, or desire for revenge against, the Japanese. 'But,' said his father, 'such suffering should never be forgotten.' And precisely that, I think, is one good reason (among many) why Lamentations is in the Bible.

a. A memorial

War memorials are erected 'lest we forget'. Of course, the intention of 'not forgetting' was so that we might never go down the same road again – a perennially forlorn longing. Nevertheless, there is a strong human instinct that when real suffering happens to whole communities it should not merely pass unnoticed into historical amnesia (or even worse, deliberate denial). And that remains true *even if* the suffering comes to an end, or achieves some good purpose, or is simply replaced by better times.

---

[11] Chatto & Windus, 2014.

We know from our biblical history that the exile ended. Some of Lady Zion's children returned. Jerusalem was rebuilt. A second temple was built. Israel survived and life went on. But that restoration does not erase the suffering of those who went through the horrors of 587 BC.[12] Lamentations, then, stands as a witness for them. It acknowledges the raw truth of what happened and refuses to allow their pain merely to evaporate with the passing of time. It compels readers for ever afterwards to look and listen, to remember and reflect.[13] 'The biblical book of Lamentations refuses denial, practices truth-telling, and reverses amnesia.'[14]

b. A voice

A war memorial on stone is a silent witness. It is in the *poetry* of the First World War that we hear the living voice of that generation, now dead to the last man and woman. Likewise the poetry of Lamentations gives voice to those who were rendered voiceless in the vortex of violence. 'What can I say for you?' asks the Poet (2:13). His whole book is the answer. He lets them speak for themselves. And that, as is well known, is a vital part of any hope for healing from deepest trauma. For intense and prolonged suffering can make people, sometimes literally, speechless. And we may want to step in with our comfort or correction, our advice and solutions. But Lamentations simply makes us listen to the voices of the sufferers – in the profusion and confusion of their pain, the bitterness of their protest, their shafts of self-condemnation, their brief flashes of hope and long night of despair, and their plaintive pleading with God just to look and see. And if in the midst of these voices there is accusation against God, Lamentations lets us hear that too, just as the books of Jeremiah and Job record their complaints and protests. This book forces us to listen to every mood that the deepest suffering causes, allowing the words that emerge to have their own integrity and authenticity, whether we approve or not. We are called not to judge, but to witness. Not to speak, but to listen. The voices of Lamentations demand the respect that is owed to honesty – the most ruthless honesty before God. 'This is what really happened,' they say. 'This is what we went through, and this is what we felt.'

---

12 Any more than the resurrection erases the suffering of the cross.

13 'The burden of Lamentations is not to question why this happened, but to give expression to the fact that it did . . . The book is not an explanation of suffering but a re-creation of it and a commemoration of it' (Berlin, p. 18).

14 O'Connor, p. 94.

c. A confession

Among those moods, among those moments of honesty, there is confession of sin. The people of Jerusalem, whether through the comments of the Poet, the groaning of Lady Zion or the corporate prayer of the whole community, acknowledge that their own rebellion and folly, uncorrected by their religious leaders, had brought upon them the wrath of God through the agency of their human enemies. Words to that effect come in every chapter. It is a theological thread running through the book (1:5, 8, 14, 18; 2:1, 14, 17; 3:39, 42; 4:6, 11, 13; 5:16).

It is, of course (and we must emphasize this immediately), a confession that is very particular. It connects the specific events of 587 BC to the equally specific record of sin and rebellion against YHWH, the covenant God of Israel, that stretched back across the centuries. It is not a theology of suffering and sin to be applied in general to any situation where people suffer. On the contrary, it is a theology of judgment governed by the covenant relationship between God and Old Testament Israel. In fact, as Jeremiah and other prophets pointed out, the catastrophe of 587 BC was not a denial of that covenant relationship, but the proof of it. It demonstrated that God meant what he said, that YHWH was as faithful to his threats as to his promises. At its inception the covenant had included sanctions – the notorious curses that would come on the people for persistent disloyalty to their covenant Lord (Lev. 26; Deut. 28).[15] In 587 BC, they came.

Two responses to this theological thread in the book seem to take us in wrong directions. One is to dismiss or minimize the idea that the suffering of Jerusalem was God's punishment for their sin, by calling it, for example, 'the conventional explanation of the events'.[16] Kathleen O'Connor considers that the book itself actually rejects or severely undermines that concept. It is articulated in 1:5 and 1:8 by the narrator. 'Not surprisingly, the narrator accepts the tradition – still common today – that suffering is divine punishment for sin . . . in chapter 1 he holds fast to the traditional interpretation of disaster.' However, in chapter 2 he draws back from this theology, and is so shocked by Lady Zion's suffering that he turns from

---

[15] '[Lamentations] assumes the "theology of destruction" in which destruction and exile are the punishment for sin (cf. Deut. 4:26–27; 28:32–67; 29:23–27; 30:17–18) . . . Why immortalize this moment of destruction? Because in its own way it signifies the truth of the Bible's theology, and it points to the continuation of the covenant between God and Israel' (Berlin, p. 18).

[16] Berlin, p. 72.

being her accuser (in ch. 1) to being her advocate, accusing God instead. God, not Judah, is the real culprit. 'He [the narrator] no longer blames her; instead, he charges God with violent abuse of city woman Zion . . . He stops impaling her with his theology of blame and retribution.'[17] So the book as a whole then becomes an *anti*-theodicy – that is, not defending the *justice* of God's ways, but accusing God of blatant *injustice*.

Now I do not deny that there is protest and even accusation against God in Lamentations (see the next section). But my problem with this view is that its advocates seem not to have read Jeremiah, or Ezekiel, or the story of the late monarchy in Israel and Judah in 2 Kings. That is, do they take seriously the account of the depth and depravity of the nation's religious apostasy, social disintegration, economic oppression, judicial corruption, criminal violence and bloodshed, and political factions and folly? Every conceivable form of moral and spiritual wickedness was flourishing, with disastrous consequences for families, for the poor, for the victims of rampant inequality and greed, and for those caught up in the ritualized sexual abuse of the fertility cults. And all of this in a nation that claimed a covenant relationship with the living God and knowledge of his ethical standards ('the way of the LORD').[18]

And do those who see Lamentations as one great accusation against God for acting as if 'mad, out of control, swirling about in unbridled destruction',[19] reflect at all on the *patience* of God? The events of 587 BC did not happen out of the blue. There had been warning after warning, appeal after appeal – all with the longing on God's part that the judgment need not fall. Eighteen years earlier God told Jeremiah to write in a scroll all the words he had spoken for the past twenty-three years, in the hope that 'Perhaps when the people of Judah hear about every disaster I plan to inflict on them, they will each turn from their wicked ways; then I will forgive their wickedness and their sin' (Jer. 36:3). King Jehoiakim burnt that scroll, setting his kingdom on a downward course that led inexorably to the inferno of 587 BC. And for many generations before that, God had

---

[17] O'Connor, pp. 21, 33, 107.

[18] 'Readers who come into Lamentations from Jeremiah . . . will enter chapter 1 with a strong and clear view of the enormity of the sin of Jerusalem, something the whole book of Jeremiah testifies to and develops . . . They will *not* be inclined to see the acknowledgment of sin as mere lip service, but as reminders of Judah's deep and sustained depravity depicted in Jeremiah' (Parry, pp. 161–162). That has been my own route, having come to work on this exposition of Lamentations after six years working on *The Message of Jeremiah*, BST (Nottingham: IVP, 2014; rev. edn, London: IVP, 2023).

[19] O'Connor, p. 33.

warned the people through the prophets – right up to the reign of their last king – that the covenant curses would no longer be mere words on a scroll but would fall upon them in horrific reality. Their sin and folly, their covenantal unfaithfulness and international scheming, would bounce back and devour them through the implacable jaws of the monster of Babylon. In the end, all the warnings were unheeded, and so the disaster happened. And Lamentations knows it, which is why the remorse is so bitter.

But the other inadequate response to the confession of sin in Lamentations is, at the opposite extreme, to claim that it completely explains everything. So we can read the horrific accounts of all the violence, destruction and suffering, and simply say, 'It was all God's punishment for their sin.' And then we can close the book with grim satisfaction that the moral balance of the universe is intact – 'they got what they deserved'. But that, surely, is to fail to listen to the agonized voices in the book, when they surround their honest acknowledgment of their own sin with honest questioning of what today would be called the 'proportionality' of the suffering inflicted on them by Babylon in the 'day of God's anger'. Robin Parry puts the point well:

The implicit complaint against God in the book is that the punishment seems to exceed the crime. It is too deep, cutting the nation to the heart. It is too wide, taking in innocent children. It lasts too long . . . This may be a just punishment *when considered at a group level*, but when we consider the impact on individuals it is clear that it is an imperfect justice. The righteous suffer alongside the guilty (Ezek. 21:3–4). That is the issue with the suffering children; they did not sin, yet they suffer terribly. Whatever God is doing in the destruction, saying that it is a punishment for sin is an inadequate theodicy, *even if it is true*. No adequate theodicy is given in this book or anywhere else in the Bible. It never tells us why the people suffer for as long as they do or in the way that they do, why the righteous are killed, or why the children starve to death in the laps of their mothers.[20]

---

[20] Parry, pp. 202–203 (emphasis original). This takes us, of course, to the vexed issue of the nature and origin of evil as such, and whether the Bible ever provides an answer to the question 'Where and how did evil originate within God's good creation?' I have wrestled with that issue, and come to the conclusion that it does not, in *The God I Don't Understand: Reflections on Tough Questions of Faith* (Grand Rapids: Zondervan, 2008).

d. A protest

The 'Why?' will not go away, however, and when it is raised up to God it emerges as protest. This is a note that we also find in some of the psalms of lament, and of course in the books of Jeremiah and Job. When people with faith in God experience or witness the realities of injustice, oppression, violence, lying, and all the suffering they cause, they cry out to God in protest. Why do such things happen?

It is important to recognize that such protest is not in itself *blaming* God for doing wrong. Nor, in my view, is it intrinsically sinful. It is faith seeking understanding. If God rules the world, and if God is the God of justice and compassion (as we affirm that he does and is), why does he permit such evil to persist? Such protest, in other words, is not a *denial* of God's sovereignty, let alone of God's existence. Rather, it *assumes* the sovereignty and goodness of God, and on that foundation is bold to hold up before God the realities of our lives that seem to contradict and undermine that very foundation. Protest to God is also protest *for* God – that is, it emerges from a passionate concern for God's name to be vindicated in the midst of all that slanders it. The voice of protest firmly believes that the Judge of all the earth will do right (Gen. 18:25), but longs for reassurance that ultimately he *will indeed* do so, unmistakeably and visibly. In the meantime, the struggle goes on, and the protesting questions remain. That is the essence of biblical lament. It is faith struggling with vertigo over the chasm between what it knows to be true about God and the realities of what it sees or experiences in this fallen world.

Such vertigo becomes even more threatening and protest-worthy when the relationship between God and Israel is considered. 'Who is it that you are treating like this?' asks Lady Zion (2:20; my own translation).

> If God rescues, liberates, and protects as their cherished biblical story tells them, how could such events occur? If God dwells with them in the Jerusalem temple, if God makes covenants with them to be their God, then how could these things happen?[21]

Well, the prophets could provide some answers, as we have seen. But could anything justify Babylon's smashing the whole nation to pieces with all the death and destruction involved?

---

[21] O'Connor, p. 7.

Lamentations accepts both the sovereignty of God, and the righteous wrath of God that is his justified reaction to persistent, unrepented sin. It recognizes, however, that God's judgment can operate through the agency of human beings who, in executing God's judgment at the 'street level' of history, are themselves guilty of the most appalling wickedness and cruelty, even against the relatively innocent in the community. In the catastrophe of 587 BC, all of these elements clash together in the conflagration. God is sovereign; God is judge. But even so, 'Why, Lord? How long, O Lord?' Significantly, the book ends by putting these things together in adjacent verses. The voice of faith proclaims God's sovereignty (in a surprising outburst, in view of all that has just been said immediately before):

> You, LORD, reign for ever;
>   your throne endures from generation to generation.
> (5:19)

And then the voice of protest immediately follows, as if to say, 'That being so . . .'

> *Why* do you always forget us?
>   *Why* do you forsake us so long?
> (5:20; my italics)

The very character of God is thrown into the furnace of human suffering in the book of Lamentations. God is exposed to enormous challenge as to what he has inflicted on Judah at the hands of her enemies – even when his anger is acknowledged as his just response to their rebellion. Yet God emerges as the ultimately faithful and compassionate one, who, even when he afflicts people in judgment, does not do so 'from his heart'. God is the one to whom you bring your anger, pain and protest. God is also the one to whom you bring your penitence and prayer. And God is the one in whom alone your hope can be ultimately secure, however long it is delayed.

e. A home and a bottle

The specific context of Lamentations, as we have emphasized, is the destruction of Jerusalem in 587 BC, interpreted as the outworking of God's judgment on the covenant nation of Israel after generations of unfaithfulness on their part and warnings on God's part. That is the very clear theological understanding of the reason behind the suffering that generation endured in that event, even if, as we agree, it is not a sufficient explanation or justification for the extent of the suffering and its apparent unfairness in swallowing up women and children, old and young, in its jaws.

But there is a very great deal of suffering in our world. And most of it cannot and should not be interpreted in the way Lamentations interprets 587 BC.[22] Nevertheless, it seems to me that Lamentations can provide a valid response. If the book voices the pain of those who knowingly suffered under the judgment of God, how much more does it speak for those who suffer for all kinds of other reasons – in inexplicable disasters, as refugees and 'collateral damage' in the endless wars of humanity, under persecution for the name of Christ, and many more. The imagery of the book captures so many scenes of suffering in our world, and the voices of the book express the turmoil of anger, shame, grief, abandonment, humiliation and protest that such suffering generates. The book is an authentic portrayal of realities that many in our world today still endure. The brutality and the misery go on and on.

For that reason, the book provides, in Kathleen O'Connor's very apt phrase, 'a house for sorrow and a school for compassion'.[23] Lamentations is a home for the sufferer. It provides the safe space, the rooms, in which grief can be expressed to its limits, over and over again, without interruption or denial, even if without comfort as yet. Or to change the metaphor, using the title of her book, *Lamentations and the Tears of the World*, we might think of Lamentations *for* the tears of the world.

And tears, we know, are precious to God. God sees and hears those who weep (whether he answers them immediately or not), and he does not forget their tears. There are, of course, tears of repentance (5:15–17). And there are tears of loneliness (1:16), tears of sympathy (2:11), tears of supplication (2:18–19). And they all have their own validity. 'We need to acknowledge when the tears of lament are tears of pain, frustration, and

---

[22] Other than in the broadest possible sense that suffering in this fallen world is primarily the result of human sin and collusion with satanic evil in general. We all share in the sin and guilt of our fallen condition and suffer consequences at many levels. But this is very different from alleging that specific suffering constitutes God's judgment on specific sins, in individuals or communities. Such simplistic equations are denied by the book of Job and the words of Jesus (Luke 13:1–5; John 9:1–3).

[23] O'Connor, p. 86.

anger rather than tears of pious repentance. And we need to recognize the legitimacy of such tears.'[24] For God does.

> You have kept count of my tossings;
>> put my tears in your bottle.
>> Are they not in your book?
> (Ps. 56:8, ESV)

Lamentations is that book, that bottle for the tears of the exiles, and by extension for the tears of the world. Kathleen O'Connor, referring to that psalm, captures the power of tears in a most moving way.

> The tears of Lamentations are of loss and grief, abandonment and outrage. They are a flag, a sign, a revelation of injury and destruction, an expression of resistance to the world's arrangements. Lamentations validates tears. It has the power to gather bitter pain and bring tears to the surface. Then it accepts them . . .
> God receives and tenderly holds tears as if they are precious, explosive testimony that must be preserved for some future day. Perhaps this vigilant, seeing, tear-collecting God weeps with the weeping world. Lamentations does not say this, of course, but . . . the book itself is a 'sacred bottle' for the tears of the world. It records them in a book, respects them, keeps account of them to present to God when God is ready to receive them.[25]

Actually, there is no 'perhaps' about the weeping of God. We know from Jeremiah that God weeps with his people and his prophet. We know from Isaiah that 'in all their affliction he was afflicted' (Isa. 63:9, ESV). And we also know, for we have read the rest of the Bible, that 'some future day' is not a vague longing, but the certainty of God's own promise that he will 'wipe away the tears from all faces', that 'sorrow and sighing will flee away', that 'the sound of weeping and of crying will be heard . . . no more', because 'he will wipe every tear from their eyes. There will be no more death or mourning or crying or pain, for the old order of things has passed away' (Isa. 25:8; 35:10; 65:19; Rev. 21:4).

---

[24] Parry, p. 217.

[25] O'Connor, p. 130.

3. Lamentations and the Bible

We have indeed read the rest of the Bible, and we must read Lamentations within the embrace of the canon – both the canon of the Old Testament Scriptures to which it belongs, and the canon of the whole Bible as God's word. For 'the Bible speaks today' just as much through Lamentations as through any other book in the canon.

And therein lies our first point, which is a rather precious irony.

a. From God's silence to God's word

We noted above that the one voice we never hear in Lamentations is the voice of God. God remains silent throughout. He allows the other voices to speak their A to Z, till they have said all they want or can. He does not interrupt, whether to comfort or correct, to explain or excuse. And this should surely be interpreted positively, not as divine deafness but as divine restraint. Once again, Kathleen O'Connor captures this feature most sensitively.

> The silence of God in Lamentations is inspired. By this I mean it shows brilliant restraint that breathes power into the book. If God were to speak, what could God say? . . . Israel's writers had resources to help them bring God to speech if they wanted to do so . . . God's speechlessness in Lamentations must be a calculated choice, a conscious theological decision, an inspired control by the book's composers . . . Any words from God would endanger human voices . . . Divine speaking would trump all speech.
>
> Lamentations' haunting power lies in its brutal honesty about the Missing Voice; its brilliance is that it does not speak for God . . . It prevents us sliding prematurely over suffering towards happy endings. It gives the book daring power because it honors human speech. God's absence forces us to attend to voices of grief and despair, and it can reflect, vividly or remotely, our own experiences of a silent God.
>
> Because God's voice is missing, Lamentations honors truth-telling and denies 'denial'. Human speech about suffering matters so much that Lamentations presents it in all its rawness.[26]

---

[26] O'Connor, pp. 85–86.

All of that rings true. Yet it omits what happens when we receive the book as part of the canon of Scripture. For at that moment, the One who is voiceless in the book itself turns the whole book into a part of the scriptural word through which God's voice is heard. God not only allows, but ensures that this torrential outpouring of human words, with all their pain, anger, grief and questioning, should be included within the scrolls of his own word. The irony is that we hear the voice of the voiceless God – precisely in and through listening to all the other voices in the book and attending to all they say in the light of all we know. It is a similar irony to the one Psalm 19 observes about creation, where the heavens cannot speak, yet their voice is heard worldwide. So it is with the silent God of Lamentations.

> They have no speech, they use no words;
>   no sound is heard from them.
> Yet their voice goes out into all the earth,
>   their words to the ends of the world.
> (Ps. 19:3–4)

It is as if God remains silent as the Poet and Lady Zion speak again and again, but is all the time recording their words (and collecting their tears), *not* in order to refute or rebuke, or hold their words against them at some later date, but rather to let *their* words become *his* word within the grand auditorium of Scripture as a whole. That is what it means, doctrinally, to say the book is 'inspired'. It is as if God listens to all the words of the speakers in Lamentations, but then turns to us, the readers, and says, 'You need to hear this. Hear my word as you listen to these voices of my people, my poor, sinful, shamed, suffering people.' It is not just the book that honours human speech, not just the readers who are summoned to do so. God himself does so – just as God honoured the confessions and complaints of Jeremiah and the protests and demands of Job, and the 'prayers and petitions with fervent cries and tears' of his own Son (Heb. 5:7).

b. Scripture answers scripture

God's silence in the book, then, needs to be understood in such terms, and not as if God had nothing to say. On the contrary, God had already said, and would later say again, many things for Zion's comfort. They are not included in Lamentations, for the reasons above, and because the book is what it is – a memorial and a voice for those whose *present and immediate* experience of suffering seemed overwhelming, inconsolable and interminable. That memorial and voice must stand with its own integrity. In the midst of the horrors of 587 BC, Zion felt alone, abandoned, surrounded by mocking spectators but not a single comforter, exposed, raped, shamed and trampled in the dust. Lamentations sits weeping with her there.

Other scriptures, however, minister the comfort she craved – even if she could not hear it yet. Long before, Deuteronomy had foreseen a history in which unfaithfulness would lead to the implementation of the covenant curses (as had now happened), but a history that had an open future and an open choice (Deut. 29 – 32). Beyond judgment lay the promise of future restoration. Deuteronomy 30 can thus end with an evangelistic appeal to seek God and live, a hope that undergirds the final prayer of Lamentations (5:21), even if that prayer is uttered alongside continuing lament and questions. And then, of course, several of the pre-exilic prophets, climaxing with Jeremiah himself, had foreseen and warned about what eventually happened in 587 BC, but also saw beyond it to a restoration of people and land, of temple and worship.

But above all, it is in the soaring words of Isaiah 40 – 55 that we hear the clearest answer to Lamentations. The prophet's words address the reality of the suffering of Israel in exile and summon them to hope in the coming deliverance that God would bring. Babylon would fall, and Cyrus of Persia would liberate them to return to their land and city. And at point after point, the grief of Lamentations is comforted and its questions answered. Some of these can be listed as follows,[27] but one way to feel the force of this comparison would be to take the time for a revealing exercise. Read through Lamentations in one sitting. Then immediately follow that by reading through Isaiah 40 – 55 in one sitting, and see how many times the prophet's words reflect and reverse Zion's laments.[28]

---

[27] I am greatly indebted in this section to Robin Parry's commentary, which should be consulted for a full textual and theological discussion of the relationship between Lamentations and Isaiah 40 – 55, with supporting bibliography (Parry, pp. 162–168).

[28] This raises, of course, the thorny question of the date and authorship of Isaiah 40 – 55, which we cannot address here. Clearly, if the volume of links between Lamentations and the prophetic text is taken to require textual dependence of the latter on the former, then the writer of Isaiah 40 – 55 must have had the book of Lamentations in hand, and so be historically located in the exilic period. Alternatively, one has to assume that by God's inspiration the eighth-century prophet Isaiah was enabled to deliver (and perhaps seal up, Isa. 8:16–17) a word for the people living in a future that he foretold, and to address the complaints they would make. That is the assumption of the Jewish Midrash on Lamentations: 'all the severe prophecies that Jeremiah prophesied against Israel were *anticipated* and healed by Isaiah' (Lam. Rab. 26:2), as quoted by Parry, p. 162; my italics.

- Five times Zion moans that there is no one to comfort her (1:2, 9, 16, 17, 21). The prophet announces double comfort from God, and returns to the theme again and again (Isa. 40:1–2; 49:13; 51:3, 12, 19; 52:9; 54:11).
- Lady Zion grieves for the loss and fate of her children (1:5, 20; 2:11–12, 20–22; 4:3–4, 10). The prophet foresees their return and multiplication (Isa. 49:17–18, 20–22).
- The besieged citizens of Jerusalem watched in vain for a nation to save them (4:17). The watchmen in the ruins of the city will rejoice when they see YHWH coming to do just that (Isa. 52:8).
- The roads to Jerusalem were deserted, with all the joy of pilgrims gone (1:4; 5:15). The prophet sees the returning exiles coming with joy once more to Zion (Isa. 51:11).
- Lamentations ends with Zion feeling forgotten and forsaken, under God's rejection and anger (5:20, 22). The prophet acknowledges their precise words (Isa. 49:14), and that they had indeed been true – but only for 'a brief moment' (Isa. 54:6–8).
- Zion had prayed that God would deal with her enemies as he had with her (1:21–22; 3:58–66; 4:21–22). The prophet envisages exactly that for Babylon, whose fate will, in detail, mirror Zion's in Lamentations (Isa. 47).
- Lady Zion had fallen to the ground, naked, unclean, with her sins bound round her neck, and defiled by the foreigners who had 'entered' her most sacred place (1:8–10, 14). The prophet, using the same female personification, summons her to shake off the dust, put on splendid clothes, free the chains from her neck, and be assured that she will never be entered and defiled again (Isa. 52:1–3).
- She who had been widowed and shamed (1:1) will forget that shame when YHWH her husband takes her again in marriage (Isa. 54:4–6).
- Those who had become foreigners in their own land and forced to buy their water and bread in fear (5:2, 4, 9) are promised restoration to their land (Isa. 54:2–3) and invited to the free wells, vineyard and bakery of God's salvation (Isa. 55:1–2).
- The city that had been razed to the ground, its gold and sacred stones scattered like gravel (2:1–10; 4:1), will be rebuilt in splendour with precious stones for its foundations, battlements and walls (Isa. 54:11–12).

So while we must read Lamentations for itself, giving full attention to its voices of uncomforted pain, for all the reasons given above in section 2, we cannot read it as if Isaiah 40 – 55 had not also been written. We hear it as scriptural truth in and of itself, and we also hear it within the wider truth that the rest of Scripture provides for us.[29]

c. Scripture tells the whole story

The 'wider truth that the rest of Scripture provides' is the great biblical story, from creation to new creation. It is the great drama of Scripture, with its six decisive 'acts' or stages: (1) creation; (2) the fall of humanity into rebellion and sin; (3) God's promise to Abraham and covenantal journey with Old Testament Israel; (4) the gospel events of the birth, life, teaching, death, resurrection and ascension of Jesus of Nazareth; (5) the outpouring of the Spirit and continuing mission of God's people in the Messiah to the ends of the earth; (6) the return of Christ, final judgment and new creation.

It is from that story that we know both the background and the sequel to what confronts us in Lamentations. We know of God's election of Israel in Abraham to be the means of blessing reaching all nations of humanity mired in sin and strife; God's redemption of his people from Egypt; the grace-gifts of covenant and law at Sinai; the inheritance of the land; the covenant with David; the building of the temple – and then the long sad decline into sin and rebellion in which Israel embodied and recapitulated the sin of humanity and brought upon themselves the curses that Genesis 3 and Deuteronomy 28 had announced. Lamentations sits in that accursed place, the pit of God's judgment, the place of death and destruction as evil does its worst.

But it is also from that story that we know 587 BC was not the end, either of Israel or of God's purpose through them for the world. The 'death' of exile was transformed by God's sovereign power into the 'resurrection' of the return. The death and resurrection of Christ then accomplished the ultimate defeat of the reign of sin and death, which will be completed when he returns to share his reign with a redeemed humanity in the new creation.

So keeping the whole Bible story in mind means that when we arrive in Lamentations we have an understanding of what had led up to such a

---

[29] 'The coming of YHWH to comfort does have implications for how we hear the pain of Lady Zion, for *we now know what she did not*' (Parry, p. 168; emphasis original).

portrait of sheer desolation and horror – especially if we arrive there (as I have done) after a long journey in Jeremiah's company. But it also means that as we sit listening to voices that sound as if the end of the world had come, we know that it had not. The story will go on. For this is God's story, and it is for all nations and all creation, not just Old Testament Israel.

Nevertheless, Lamentations is there. It is simply *there*, in our Bibles. Spending time in it is like pressing the pause button, freezing the action of the drama, memorializing that moment in the story when it did indeed seem as if the story itself had ended. It forces us to consider very seriously the significance of 587 BC, not only as the lowest point of Old Testament history, but as a *sign*-ificant event, one that points to the reality of God's judgment and what it meant to bear it at one point in history, and what it would mean (in symbolic terms depicting shame, aloneness, forsakenness and death) to bear it absolutely or eternally. Lamentations creates the space for reflection on the theological, spiritual and canonical import-ance of that event, reflection that will lead us in a moment to Christ himself.

So then, we must not read Lamentations without the rest of the Bible. But equally, we should not read the rest of the Bible without Lamentations (as Christians have habitually tended to do).

4. Lamentations and Christ

Come for a moment and consider another devastating disaster that engulfed a whole people. In November 2013 Typhoon Haiyan struck the Philippines. At that time it was the strongest tropical cyclone ever recorded at landfall, the strongest ever in terms of sustained wind speeds (reaching a sustained one-minute speed of 195 miles per hour). It caused cata-strophic damage, destroying whole towns and villages. It caused 6,300 confirmed deaths (with estimates of the nameless dead much higher), and rendered some one million people homeless.

One little girl managed to reach one of the evacuation centres as the typhoon came. The waters began rushing in and her mother shouted at her to go up to the second floor. At that moment she cried out this prayer: '*Jesus, tama na po!*' ('Jesus, please, enough!'). Then she felt something or someone lifting her up to safety, and she survived. A staff worker with a Christian relief effort talked with her later and heard her story. Rico Villanueva, a Langham Scholar and Old Testament teacher in the

Philippines whose seminary was deeply engaged in helping the stricken communities, relates the story and reflects on it thus:

> *'Jesus, tama na po!'* (*'Jesus, please, enough!'*).
>
> Let us pause and try to reflect on the 'theology' behind this prayer. I think we can draw out three beliefs about the disaster in relation to God from this prayer. First, God is viewed as the one causing the disaster. That is why the girl asked Jesus to stop. Secondly, the girl sees Jesus as the savior, which is why she is calling to him for help. Third, God is addressed as 'Jesus'.
>
> The first two statements seem contradictory: God cannot be both the one who brings the disaster and the one who delivers from the disaster. And yet in this prayer, the punisher[30] and the savior is one. God is both the cruel Judge and the merciful Father. This raises the question why? If God is good (savior) why is he punishing us? If he is the cruel one then why pray to him in the first place? But it appears that for this girl there is no problem with holding the two views together. How is she able to do this? I think the answer lies in the third statement above. In calling 'Jesus' instead of 'God' the girl is simply voicing out what many of our people have learned about God: that God is one with us in our sufferings through Jesus. This Filipino girl belongs to a country where the most popular image of Jesus is the crucified or suffering Christ (Jesus Nazareno). Our view of Jesus as God who is with us in our sufferings enables us to cling on to the God who is also our Savior and Father even in times of disasters.[31]

'Jesus as God who is with us' – the very meaning of 'Immanuel', a sign given at another time of crisis in Judah, and a name that, in its context then, expressed both imminent judgment and hope of deliverance (Isa. 7:1 – 8:10). That God suffers *with* his people is a biblical truth that Old

---

[30] This is the only point where I would query Villanueva's terminology. To say that God has in some sense 'caused' (or permitted) the disaster does not mean that it was an act of God's *punishment*. Of course, the little girl may have thought so, but that does not make it true! We need to distinguish carefully but emphatically between affirming the sovereignty of God within which all things occur, and God's use of natural and historical events as agents of his judgment. To affirm (with all the mystery it involves) that a typhoon happens within the realm of God's sovereignty is not to affirm that it happens as an act of God's judgment. Equally, to question the idea that natural disasters in general (or any one in particular) constitute acts of God's judgment is not to deny the sovereignty of the Lord of history and creation.

[31] Rico Villanueva, '"My God, Why?" Natural Disasters and the Response of God', an unpublished paper delivered to the Langham Partnership International Research and Training Seminar, Wycliffe Hall, Oxford, September 2014, p. 1.

Testament Israelites knew, but is there any hint of it in Lamentations? One small hint might be in the tears of 2:11, which the speaker says he pours out 'because *my people* are destroyed'. That is a very characteristic phrase of Jeremiah, used interchangeably by the prophet and by God. Do we hear the voice of God hidden behind the tears of the speaker? If the speaker is not actually Jeremiah but is speaking, as it were, with his voice, he might have in mind a remarkable piece of divine emotion in Jeremiah 42:10. God says, 'I am sorry for the disaster I have brought upon you' (NRSV) – referring precisely to the devastation of 587 BC.[32] Villanueva refers to this text in his further reflection:

> In Jer 42:10 God looks at the whole destruction of Jerusalem and feels the pain. In view of God's pathos in the whole book of Jeremiah, God seems to be saying in Jer 42:10, 'I am sorry for the disaster I have brought upon you.' The 'sorry' ought not to be understood in an apologetic sense but in [a] sympathetic sense. Even a parent who has disciplined his son can say: I am sorry for the pain you felt. God shares with the experience of those who go through disasters and feels what they feel. For us Christians we know this to be true because Christ himself suffered at the cross. We know that in Christ the contradiction in God's saving and judging his people is embraced.[33]

And that brings us to the most intriguing link between Lamentations and Christ. There is one more connection between Lamentations and Isaiah 40 – 55 that was not mentioned above, and that is the extensive verbal parallels between the experience and discourse of 'the Man' in Lamentations 3 and that of the Servant of the Lord in Isaiah – especially Isaiah 52:13 – 53:12.[34] Both figures suffer terribly, and both suffer explicitly at the hand of God. The difference is, of course, that the suffering of the Servant is finally seen as innocent (not being punished by God for his own sin), vicarious (bearing the sins of his people) and victorious. For that

---

[32] The precise meaning of *niḥam* is difficult to express here. The text is not saying that God *regrets* what he had done in judgment (as if the verse were an apology), or that he 'relented' about it (NIV, ESV) in the sense of changing his mind, for he had not – it had happened. Rather it probably expresses the grief of God, along with the fact that, now the worst had happened, God could indeed begin to deal with them differently.

[33] Villanueva, 'My God, Why?', p. 7.

[34] These are fully outlined and discussed by Parry, pp. 166–168. They include, for example, walking in darkness (Lam. 3:2; Isa. 50:10); offering to be struck on the cheek (Lam. 3:30; Isa. 50:6); remaining silent (Lam. 3:28; Isa. 53:7); being stricken, pierced, afflicted and crushed (Lam. 3:1, 13, 19, 33–34; Isa. 53:4–5); being cut off and 'buried' (Lam. 3:53–54; Isa. 53:8–9).

reason, Christians have readily seen Jesus Christ as the Servant figure (following the lead of Christ himself and the New Testament as they do so), who was 'pierced for our transgressions' and 'crushed for our iniquities', because 'the LORD has laid on him the iniquity of us all'.

But who was 'the Man'? In the poetry of Lamentations 3, he is the personified people of Judah. He speaks for them, though he also speaks *to* them (something else that he has in common with the Servant). The suffering of the whole people is concentrated, as it were, in the poetic persona of this witness and advocate.

And who was the Servant? In the prophetic texts of Isaiah, he is also the personified people of Israel as a whole. That is his identity when first introduced (Isa. 41:8). And even though it seems unavoidable (imperative indeed, in the light of the New Testament) to see the later characterization of the Servant as portraying an individual who will accomplish God's purpose *for* Israel, the Servant never loses that corporate identity *as* Israel. He stands in their place and bears their suffering, giving his life as a sacrifice for their sin.

And who is Jesus? Immanuel, *God* with us. The mystery of the incarnation is that not only did Jesus, as Messiah-King, embody *Israel's* Servant identity, he also, as Lord, embodied YHWH, Israel's God. 'God was reconciling the world to himself in Christ' (2 Cor. 5:19). In Christ, therefore, and supremely of course at the cross, God entered into the reality of the suffering of the world. But not only as an act of empathy or sympathy, but redemptively, taking upon himself the whole burden of sin and evil, human and satanic, that underlies that suffering. At the cross, God bore in himself, in the person of his Son, the reality of God's own judgment against sin.

When we connect the death of Christ to the Old Testament, as Paul tells us we should,[35] we can see the destruction of Jerusalem in 587 BC as a portent of the cross (both of them acts of human wickedness that were simultaneously the outpouring of God's judgment), and the return from exile as a portent of the resurrection (and ultimately, in longer prophetic vision, of the new creation). And as we read Lamentations again in the light of that connection, the experiences of Lady Zion (especially in Lam. 1) and the Man (in 3:1–18) find multiple echoes in the passion of Christ.

---

[35] When Paul writes, 'Christ died for our sins in accordance with the scriptures' (1 Cor. 15:3, NRSV), he does not mean we can look up the story in the Gospel accounts. They were not written yet. He means the scriptures of the Old Testament. And he means that the death of Christ should be interpreted within the framework of the story and the promise of the whole Old Testament canon.

Jesus not only wept, like Lady Zion, over Jerusalem, but like her he also suffered desertion by his friends, mockery from his enemies, and apathy from passers-by. Like her, he was stripped naked, publicly exposed and humiliated, with none to comfort. Like her, he suffered all this at the hands of an implacable foreign enemy wielding idolatrous imperial power through blood and brutality. Was there, indeed, any suffering like his, that the Lord laid on him in the day of his fierce anger? Like her, he became unclean, defiled by sin that was not his own, but because God made him to be sin for us. And in that state of sin and uncleanness even God could not look on him. That awful cry of dereliction wrenched from Psalm 22, 'My God, my God, why have you forsaken me?', speaks the unspeakable mystery of divine abandonment, which was for Christ a depth of suffering, a hell, more infinite than Lady Zion or the psalmist could imagine. And at that moment too, God refrained from answering – as in Lamentations. On that occasion, the silence of God spoke the redemption of creation.

And like the Man (if Christ could take the lament of Ps. 22 on his lips, might the metaphors of Lam. 3:1–18 not also have spoken for him?), Christ felt the blows of a rod, the tearing of his flesh, the impotence of an inescapable 'prison' on the cross, piercing, mockery, bitterness and gall. Like the Man, too, however, Christ could and did entrust himself to the God of ultimate faithfulness and compassion, knowing that he would not be 'cast off for ever'. Jesus died in agony, no doubt. But he did not die in despair.

Reading Lamentations, then, in the light of Christ does not mean that we simply jump straight to Jesus and make it all speak about the cross, or hastily make it all right in the end because of the resurrection. We must not short-circuit the book like that. We must let it speak for itself, and for those whose voices the Poet brings to our ears. But it does mean that in the sufferings of Jerusalem – both in the sense that they were deserved and to the extent that they were not – we see a glimpse in advance of the sufferings of the One who took on himself not only the identity of Israel but also the sins of the world.

And here, then, is another way in which the silent God of the book is actually speaking within it as part of his word. For in the voices of Lamentations we hear not only the voice of suffering Israel, not only by extension the voice of a suffering world, but also the voice of the suffering divine Son of God, whose death and resurrection brings salvation to both.

5. Lamentations and the church

Finally, what message can Lamentations have for the Christian church? We might begin to answer that by asking where we see ourselves in the book. The traditional and impulsive answer is to identify ourselves with the victims, the people of God suffering at the hands of violent enemies. But we must start from a more uncomfortable perspective.

a. 'First to the Jew'

Lamentations spoke first for the suffering of Old Testament Israel at the hands of their enemies. For that reason, it has been read and used liturgically by Jewish people all down the centuries, as a response to the long history of such suffering – not only at the hands of the Babylonians and Romans, but tragically also at the hands of people and powers claiming to be Christian. The story of Christian anti-Semitism is one of the darkest stains on the face of the church, and, because of the suffering it has caused, it should not be forgotten, any more than Lamentations lets us forget 587 BC. This perspective makes us read Lamentations and see ourselves among those enemies who inflicted such humiliation and pain on Israel.

> Hearing Lamentations as a text by Jews and for Jews[36] in which Gentile Christian believers have often shamefully enacted the role of the destructive nations would actually be one very constructive, chastening reading strategy . . .
>
> It does not take much knowledge of Jewish–Christian relations throughout history to see how Lamentations might serve to expose past Christian acts for what they are. We need to . . . acknowledge the legitimacy of that interpretation – *legitimacy retained within a Christian theological frame of reference.* If we who are Christians are not prepared to face our history and to allow Scripture to expose our infidelity, then what claims do we have to honor and tremble before God's word?[37]

b. 'Blessed are the peacemakers'

And if that rings true to the history of anti-Semitism, it speaks no less powerfully to all other contexts in which the Christian church has aligned

---

[36] Even allowing for the anachronism that it is probably inappropriate to use the term 'Jews' for the people of Israel at this stage of their biblical history, I think Parry's point stands.

[37] Parry, pp. 175–176.

itself, in reality or in its rhetoric, with imperial power, military aggression, colonial greed and sometimes genocidal violence – from the post-Constantinian Roman Empire, through the Crusades, the conquistadores, slavery, the church's preaching in support of the First World War (on both sides), and even the rhetoric of some churches around the 2003 invasion of Iraq.[38] The story of Christian complicity in wars, violence and bloodshed is another of the scandalous blemishes on the bride of Christ, which only his return will wash away.

But Lamentations blows away any sentimental or sanitized imaginings we might have about what war is. War is hell on earth and Lamentations shows it in grisly detail. It assaults our ears with the noise of battle, the screams of dying soldiers and of women systematically raped as an instrument of war, and the deathly groaning silence that follows such desolation. It assaults our eyes with scenes of awesome material destruction of buildings, fortifications and homes, the raging inferno of a whole city on fire, the horrors of starvation and cannibalism, and the desperate humiliating struggle for survival. It arouses our outrage at the desecration of holy sites, the suffering of mothers and children and the elderly, and systematic torture and abuse. All of this in 587 BC, and still with us today. Lamentations is surely an exposure of the ghastly horror of war – even when it acknowledges that in that instance it was a human tragedy that mediated divine judgment. Should such things happen? asks Lady Zion (2:20–22). Surely God's answer and ours has to be: No, they should not.

It would be hard to claim that Lamentations on its own demands radical pacifism as an ethical ideology,[39] but it certainly reinforces Christ's call to (and blessing upon) peacemaking as a missional responsibility. Anything that Christians, individually or collectively, can do, in ministries of reconciliation and conflict resolution, to prevent such diabolical barbarity and atrocity surely carries the endorsement of the Prince of Peace.

And since warfare is a particular habit and pride of empires, Lamentations also stands as a critique of the kind of imperial violence represented by Babylon – a critique that reaches epic proportions in

---

[38] Daniel Berrigan scourges the idolatrous militarism of the West, and the complicity of many Christian leaders. 'In Lamentations, the Christian default also stands revealed. American religion, in the purview of the American empire, provokes no quarrel, no questioning. Instead of uttering a prophetic outcry, the leaders fall in line. By compliant silence and complicit word, the Church shows herself reliable, a collaborator – the god is on our side' (p. 17).

[39] Though Daniel Berrigan certainly turns it into a powerful anti-war tract, in his searing exposition of it in the wake of 9/11 and the subsequent bombing of Afghanistan.

Jeremiah 50 – 51. What Babylon did to Jerusalem is what empires do to those who resist them – until God brings his own justice to bear in the end, as he did in the exodus and as he always will, right up to the final justice and great hallelujah of Revelation 18 – 19. There is a prophetic stance for the church in perceiving this biblical theme and bearing costly witness to it, including within the political sphere. This too is part of our missional response to the book.

> Readers are invited to bring political calamity into God's presence and to seek salvation; they are encouraged to look with merciful eyes at victims of political violence even if those victims are not 'innocent'; they are encouraged to see political evil for what it is and to speak its name; they are guided towards becoming honest-to-God lamenters, God-dependent pray-ers who hunger and thirst for righteousness, who refuse the political violence of empire, and who pray 'Your kingdom come, your will be done, on earth as it is in heaven.'[40]

c. 'Weep with those who weep'

But we must attend to the primary voices of the book – the suffering victims who cry out in their desolation for God to look and see. And they do so as the people who know their God and who had a thousand-year history that demonstrated from its beginning that YHWH is the God of compassion who hears the cries of the oppressed and looks on their misery – and then steps in as their deliverer and champion. In the middle of the book, there will be some reassurance that God will do again what he has done before (3:52–58). But at first, throughout chapters 1 and 2, no such divine attention or action greets their pleas.

Who then *will* look and see? Who will come alongside to comfort? The book is a direct address to the reader to fulfil that role or be condemned as a passer-by worse than the priest and Levite in Jesus' parable.

> Is it nothing to you, all you who pass by?
>> Look around and see.
> Is any suffering like my suffering
>> that was inflicted on me . . . ?
> (1:12)

---

[40] Parry, 'Lamentations and the Poetic Politics of Prayer', p. 88.

And so the book assigns to us, as Christian readers, the missional task of hearing the voice of the oppressed and persecuted, bearing witness to their suffering, and advocating on their behalf – which is part of the purpose and power of lament. This we must do, of course, as the New Testament instructs us, primarily on behalf of sisters and brothers in Christ who suffer for his name. The catalogue of places where such suffering is rampant would be too long to list here, but certainly includes Christians in Syria and Iraq, North Africa, Nigeria, Sudan, North Korea, some Central Asian states, Sri Lanka, and many other places.

But weeping with those who weep is surely not confined to shedding and sharing Christian tears. Lamentations gives us tears for the world – a world weeping over the millions of deaths by disease: HIV/AIDS, Ebola, malaria and preventable childhood diseases. A world of grinding poverty and hunger, now even afflicting rich nations because of gross and obscene inequality. A world of mothers grieving over the deaths of sons and husbands, whether in the wake of rockets and suicide bombs in Israel, or reprisal shelling in Gaza. A world of insane and endemic tribal and ethnic slaughter in South Sudan, Democratic Republic of Congo and even parts of Europe and Eurasia. A world of accelerating creational damage and climate change that threatens the poorest and weakest most. A world in which 2014 was deemed by several agencies to be the worst year ever for children – abused, abducted, raped, mutilated, enslaved, forced into child armies, murdered and traumatized in mass shootings in schools, from the USA to Nigeria to Pakistan, and driven by war or hunger from their homes in their thousands to wretched refugee camps.

Lamentations not only gives us the language for lament in such a world; surely it also demands that we use it. For lament appeals beyond the world and its tragic fallenness to the One about whom even Lamentations can say,

You, LORD, reign for ever;
>   your throne endures from generation to generation.
>(5:19)

Lament is missional because it keeps the world before God, and it draws God into the world – with the longing that God should act, and the faith that he ultimately will.

d. 'Therefore I have hope' (Lam. 3:21)

We may have sung 'Great Is Thy Faithfulness' without any awareness of the surrounding darkness and desolation of the Lamentations text from which it is drawn. But now that we do know that context, there is no reason not to go on singing it! For its truth is also a truth embedded in Lamentations. There is hope in this book, not just because it is set within the whole Bible story with its redemptive heart and glorious climax, but because the book is saturated with prayer. Even when it is angry, pain-soaked, protesting, grieving, questioning prayer, it is prayer anyway. And it is prayer addressed to the Lord – the God whose faithfulness, love and compassion are eternal, and whose anger, though real and terrible, will not last for ever.

And in that God, the Poet places his hope while still in the midst of his pain, and calls us to do the same.

Lamentations 1:1–22

1. No comforter

Perhaps it's because I'm a man, but I find few things more emotionally moving than a woman in tears, sobbing out some desperate pain or loss. Perhaps only the tears of a seriously injured or bereaved child are more unbearable. This chapter assaults the eyes and ears of our imagination with both a weeping woman and destitute children. The Poet presents the city of Jerusalem as a woman in the deepest depths of mourning and pain. In the first half of the chapter (1–11), he describes her in the third person in the midst of the calamity that has torn her life to shreds. In the second half (12–22), he lets the city-woman speak for herself. He has no choice; the woman interrupts his narration with her plaintive cry – first to God and then to anybody passing by (which includes us, the readers) – to look and see her suffering. At that point it is *we* who have no choice – except to stop reading. For to read is to see. And in the act of reading and seeing, *we* at least (we the readers) respond to the woman's plea for somebody to pay attention to her.

But will God pay attention? We are given no answer to that question, for God remains silent. God says nothing, in this chapter or in the whole of the rest of the book, apart from the single recollected word of 3:57. We may well want to rush in and answer for him, since our biblical memories will quickly supply plenty of God-speech from elsewhere to fill the silence. Even the Poet gets close to that in chapter 3, with theological reflections that seem to take words from God's mouth. But the God who so spectacularly answered Job stays silent in this book. Perhaps we will *have* to speak on his behalf, especially if we choose to preach the book for what it now is – part of God's word. But first we must appreciate 'the sound of silence' as God's intentional restraint.[1] It is because God refuses to interrupt that we hear the voices of the Poet and the personified Lady Zion in all their screaming anguish, groaning remorse and whispered grief. We need to follow God's example and let their voices be fully heard before we impose our own voice claiming to be his.

We should note some striking features of the poetry of this whole opening chapter before we explore the detail.

- Five times we hear the desolate refrain, *no one to comfort*. Three times the Poet says it about Jerusalem (2, 9, 17), and twice Lady Zion says it about herself (16, 21). And once more: *no one to help her* (7). It is a terrifying loneliness and culturally shocking. For grief in Israel's world was always a communal thing. Mourners gathered to wrap the bereaved in the comfort of shared grief. To be denied such comfort at the time it was most desperately needed compounded the pain to infinity.[2] By repeating this note of comfortlessness, the Poet recruits the readers to reach out and comfort this abject woman. But ultimately the appeal is to God, for in the end only God can (and will) comfort her (Jer. 31:13; Isa. 40:1; 51:12; 52:9). But we do not hear that word yet.

- Five times we hear the deathly sound of *groaning*: from the priests (4), the city (8), all her people (11) and Lady Zion (21, 22). The chapter begins in tears and ends in groans. 'Lamentations opens upon a universe of sorrow.'[3] The word 'groaning' reminds us of the Hebrews in Egypt, groaning under their hard labour. Back then, God 'heard', 'remembered' and 'looked' (Exod. 2:23–25). This chapter gives us no such reassurance, but the hope of it will surface later in the book (3:59–61).

- The most repeated word in the chapter is the word *all* – seventeen times altogether. Its negative repetition tolls the totality of Zion's tragedy. It embraces, for example, *all her lovers . . . all her friends* (2); *all who pursue her* (3); *all her gateways* (4); *all the splendour* (6); *all who honoured her* (8); *all her people* (11); *all the warriors*

---

[1] See the Introduction, section 3a, pp. 24–25.

[2] Jeremiah's loneliness involved being excluded from sharing in times of community grief (Jer. 16:5–7). Ezekiel was compelled to cope with the death of his wife without the customary mourning rites (Ezek. 24:15–24). The experience of both prophets symbolized the reality that engulfed Jerusalem.

[3] O'Connor, p. 17.

(15); *all my enemies* (21); and most threatening of all, *all my sins* (22).

> Every problem that Jerusalem faces is stated in terms of totality. The people face total oppression by enemies, total loss of property, total loss of cultic activity, total loss of leaders, total lack of sympathy from their formal allies, total surrender of prestige and dignity and total guilt before God for their sins. All weaknesses have been exposed, and all hope for avoiding catastrophe has been dashed.[4]

• Three times Lady Zion calls out to God, *Look, Lord . . .* (9, 11, 20),[5] and once to the heedless passers-by (12). Perhaps 'calls out' is too strong. A woman sitting in the dust, disgraced, despised and deserted – a woman stretching out her hands like an imploring victim of some devastating horror (17) – such a woman can probably manage only a feeble croak, a hoarse whimper squeezed out between the sobs and groans: 'Look at me, I beg you, please, won't you at least *look* at me . . .' But it is the plea that the Poet forces us to hear, and in hearing, forces us to look at what we can scarcely bear to see.[6] Whether *God* will hear and look, we do not yet know. But *our* eyes and ears must now follow the Poet's pointing finger.

1. Zion's calamity (1:1–11)

'Êkâ! The first word of the book (which is also the book's title in the Hebrew canon) is really a self-standing exclamation of lament, not just the opening word of the sentence (*How deserted . . .*). No English word quite captures it, though the older 'Alas!' came close. 'Oh!' and 'Ah!' are too trivial. The common rendering 'How . . . !' treats it as an exclamation, but the word also contains an element of questioning: 'How? Why?' It stands at the head of the three darkest chapters in the book (1, 2 and 4), and it carries a

---

[4] House, p. 342.

[5] *See* (v. 20) in the niv is the same Hebrew word as *Look* in vv. 9 and 11.

[6] 'We cannot bear to look but we cannot turn our eyes away. The more we look, the more we shame her by seeing that which should not be seen. But we must look, for the poet calls upon us to see what has happened to the city and to partake in her suffering. We become actors in the "drama" of this chapter' (Berlin, p. 48).

sense of 'How come? How can this possibly have happened?' This is baffled pain, astonished suffering, lament mingled with protest, disbelief and questions.

a. Turned upside down (1:1–3)

We are immediately introduced to the portrait of the city of Jerusalem as a woman by the feminine verb that opens the book: 'She sits alone, the city once full of people' (1a, my translation). The picture of stark reversal (from thronging crowds to deserted streets) is carried through the first three verses. That is a common theme in laments – whether for individuals, cities or empires. David's classic lament for Saul and Jonathan – 'How are the mighty fallen!' (2 Sam. 1:19, 25, 27, KJV) – has entered the English language as a proverb. The predicted fall of Babylon is likewise pictured as the humiliation of a once-proud queen, while the collapse of the empires of Tyre and Egypt are also portrayed as massive reversals from glory and power to shame and weakness (Isa. 47; Ezek. 27 – 30). Such, says the Poet, is now the fate of Jerusalem.

'Dwelling alone' (1; *how deserted lies . . .*), in Hebrew, could describe a position of protected security, such as Balaam perceived about Israel under the eye of YHWH (Num. 23:9). But it could also be the sad situation of a person with leprosy, segregated from all human company (Lev. 13:46). It is the latter that now fits Jerusalem. Once *full of people*, she is now *deserted*. Once *great among the nations*, she is as lonely as a *widow*. Once a *queen among the provinces*, she has been put to forced labour like a *slave*.

The shock of such reversal produces inconsolable weeping through the lonely night (2a) – not that anyone is there to console in any case. For whereas she had abundant *lovers* and *friends* in the past, they offer no comfort now (2b). They have mutated into traitors and enemies (2c). And few things are more painful than betrayal by friends (Pss 38:11; 55:12–14; 88:18).

The mention of *lovers* is a puzzle. A woman would have friends and neighbours of course (the word in v. 2c covers both), who would be expected to crowd around to comfort in a time of mourning. But *lovers*? Where is this woman's husband? Ah, but she is a *widow* (1b). So has her husband died? Or has he too deserted her? And if the latter, could that be because of her unfaithfulness with *lovers*? Whatever the reason, no husband is there to protect or to comfort. The husband's absence, like

God's silence (amounting to the same thing), sharpens her pain. Her aloneness is total.

Shifting from the metaphor to the theological reality it portrays: we know that the covenant relationship between YHWH and Israel was portrayed as the exclusive marriage commitment of husband and wife to each other. Both Hosea and Jeremiah make bold use of this picture – positively and negatively. So, following the metaphor, when Israel went after other gods than YHWH, or sought protective and politically advantageous alliances with other nations (which would include honouring their gods), rather than trusting solely in the covenant promises of YHWH, their unfaithfulness was portrayed as a form of spiritual adultery and prostitution. The *lovers*, in the language of the prophets, were the gods and governments of surrounding nations. And indeed, in and after the fall of Jerusalem in 587 BC, they not only failed to come to her aid, but even took advantage of her collapse.

That much we, the readers, know from the books of the prophets. But is the Poet implying all that in his laconic *all her lovers*? Is he hinting that this woman's suffering is the result of her own culpable promiscuity? If so, the complaint of 2c hides a horrid irony: she accuses them of betraying her (as she does again in v. 19), while it was she who had betrayed her divine Husband by taking them as lovers in the first place. Or is verse 2 simply a rhetorical poetic picture of utter abandonment, of Jerusalem deserted by all who should have been her friends? We get a clearer answer in verse 5, but verse 2 simply raises the question and drops the hint.[7]

If verse 1 is a reversal of status, and verse 2 a reversal of expectations, verse 3 is a reversal of history. *Affliction and harsh labour* are words strongly associated with the exodus – or rather, with the condition of the Israelites in Egypt before the exodus. But whereas in that story suffering was followed by deliverance, now the opposite has happened. 'Out of the frying pan into the fire': after more than a decade of struggling with Babylonian oppression, including the final months of siege, Judah has not gone free, but *gone into exile*.[8] And whereas, when the Egyptians pursued the

---

[7] Most commentators affirm that the Poet's use of *lovers* implies the fact of covenant unfaithfulness, and is therefore an implied accusation of the sin that lies behind the present state of Jerusalem. Iain Provan (p. 36), however, believes this is reading too much into v. 2, where the emphasis is simply on the terrible trauma itself. The word 'lovers' in English has a pejorative sense that is not necessarily there in the Hebrew participle 'those who love her'.

[8] Although the reality of the Babylonian exile is, in most people's view, the undoubted background to the book, the word itself seems almost too painful to mention. This is its only occurrence in the book – apart from 4:22, where, amazingly, Jerusalem is promised that her exile will come to an end.

fleeing Israelites, they failed and were themselves destroyed (Exod. 14), this time *all who pursue her have overtaken her* (3c). The ultimate goal of the exodus had been that God would give his people 'rest' in a land of their own – a goal accomplished (provisionally at least, as Heb. 4 reminds us) by Joshua and later to a greater extent by David (Deut. 12:9–10; Josh. 11:23; 2 Sam. 7:1, 11). But now, expelled from the land and scattered among the nations, *she finds no resting place* (3b). History has gone into reverse. The people whom God had brought out of captivity into the land are now thrown out of the land and back into captivity.

But verse 3 throws out even stronger hints that there is more to this tragedy than the misfortunes of international upheaval. The covenant between God and Israel was sanctioned by threats as well as promises, curses as well as blessings. And among the curses by which God had warned Israel of the dangers of covenant disobedience were precisely what verse 3 describes – scattering among the nations and finding no rest anywhere, but only 'an anxious mind, eyes weary with longing, and a despairing heart' (Deut. 28:64–67) – the very fabric of Lamentations.

b. Emptied out (1:4–6)

The weeping woman is named at last. But not, initially, by the geographical name of the city – Jerusalem (which is first used in v. 7). Rather, she is called *Zion* (4), or *Daughter Zion* (6). Zion means Jerusalem as the centre of the worship of YHWH, God of Israel. Zion is the place where the temple of God brought the people of God together. Zion is the place of God's presence in the midst of his people's worship. But now Zion suffers God's absence. And Zion's worship, lacking both people and place, has come to an end.

So in another bold personification, the Poet pictures the *roads to Zion* and the city gates mourning their own loss (4). Once they would have resounded with the feet and voices of throngs of pilgrims on the way into Jerusalem to worship at the temple. But now that the temple has been destroyed, all its rich and symbolic rituals are gone, and the very stones of the streets and gates lament their emptiness. *Priests* and young female singers raise their voices now, not in hymns of praise but in groans of mourning. It is indeed *bitter* for the city (4c).[9] To feel just how bitter, glance through Psalms 48, 84, 122 and 125, and sense the immense joy

---

[9] *Bitter* is the same word that Naomi chose for herself in the 'emptiness' of her triple bereavement of husband and sons (Ruth 1:20–21).

that Israelites had in participating in the worshipping life of the temple. Then contrast that with the grief that even a temporary cessation of worship during an enemy invasion caused, as reflected in Joel 1:8–13. How much more devastating was the destruction of the temple itself!

But who had done it? At one level, it was obvious: *her foes* (5a). They had triumphed[10] and now seemed to be enjoying the *ease* and peace they had so ruthlessly destroyed for Israel. But as Jeremiah had so persistently said, behind the hammer of Babylon stood the hand of God. And now for the first time the Poet makes a point that the book will ruthlessly and relentlessly affirm – in the teeth of all the pain and questions it generates. Why had the enemies triumphed over Israel? Because[11] *the LORD has brought her grief* (5b; 'afflicted her' [ESV]; 'made her suffer' [NRSV]). YHWH stands emphatically as the subject of the verb, and the reason for his action follows at once: *because of her many sins* (Heb. 'on account of the multitude of her sins'). So the hints of verses 2 and 3 are now explicit. The suffering of Lady Zion is suffering under the judgment of her covenant Lord. The word *sins* here is *pešaʿ*. It is the word frequently used by the prophets for the sin of covenant rebellion, the deliberate breaking of the sacred commitments that were built into the relationship between Israel and YHWH. It occurs three times in this chapter: first affirmed by the Poet (5), and then admitted by the desolate city-woman herself (14, 22). Her suffering is beyond imagining, but not beyond explanation. It is unbearable, but it is not innocent.

But the Poet cannot dwell on the theology of that just yet. It is the suffering itself that floods back to fill the frame. The city has been emptied of its worship (4), its little *children* (5c), its *splendour* (6a) and its leaders (6b–c). And worse is to follow.

c. Shamed and violated (1:7–10)

The Poet enters the tortured mind of the city-woman, Jerusalem, probing her memory (7a). It is filled with the pain of nostalgia and remorse when

---

[10] This is another echo of the curses of Deut. 28. That foreigners would 'become the head' (Heb.), and that Israel's little children ('suckling infants', 5c) would be taken captive, are among the catalogue of miseries foreseen in Deut. 28:41, 44.

[11] The NIV omits the word 'because' (see ESV, NRSV), which is regrettable since it stands emphatically in the Hebrew of v. 5b as the explanation of why Israel's enemies have triumphed. It is an important point. The enemies had not triumphed by their own superior power, or because YHWH had slipped up. No, as Deut. 32 had foreseen and Jeremiah so strongly insisted, Israel's human enemies were tools in the hand of their real enemy at that point in their history – their offended covenant God.

she *remembers all the treasures that were hers. Treasures* is a general word that can mean anything that is very precious. In verse 10 it clearly refers to the physical treasures of the temple. But in verse 7 it probably means everything that Israel held dear: the privilege of her covenant relationship with the living God; the gift of God's law; the gift of the land; her history of God's blessing; the temple and all that went on there; her annual festivals; her kings, priests and prophets. All of these seemed to have been swept away in the cataclysm of 587 BC.

And in place of whatever pride she once had in those precious things, she is now overwhelmed with humiliation and shame – the main theme of these verses. Defeat by enemies was (and still is) shameful (7b), and in a culture shaped by the polarity of shame and honour, the shame of defeat was doubled by the deliberate mockery of those enemies. Here we meet someone who actually does 'look' at the city-woman, but it is a lewd, gloating, unwanted look, filled with contemptuous laughter – exulting in *her destruction* (7c).

But *her destruction*, we have just been told (5b), is because of her sin, and the Poet reinforces that once more (8a). Her shame, therefore, is the product of her sin – a response as old as the garden of Eden (Gen. 3:7–10). Once again, however, the Poet focuses not so much on the magnitude of the sin as on the magnitude of humiliation and unbearable disgrace that the woman is now exposed to. She has *become unclean*. The last word of 8b is uncertain, and it may be better translated 'she has become an object of mockery or derision'.[12] And that mockery, from those who once *honoured her*, has now become even more sinister – *for they have all seen her naked[ness]* (8b). What is going on here?

In the surrounding cultures, a woman caught in adultery could be publicly shamed by having her skirts pulled up to expose her genital nakedness in public – before an even worse fate awaited. The horrors of such punishment form part of the searing imagery of Ezekiel 23. The Poet here implies an excruciating irony: the *lovers* of verse 2, with whom the city-woman had indulged her promiscuity, now humiliate her with

---

[12] The word *nîdâ* is similar to, but not identical with, *niddâ* – which refers to a menstruating woman who was ritually (but not morally) unclean (cf. Lev. 12:2, 5; 15:19–33). To have sexual intercourse with ('uncover the nakedness of') a menstrual woman was also prohibited as unclean (Lev. 20:18). Many scholars, noting the mention of nakedness in 8b, consider this word *nîdâ* a variant, or a copying error, for *niddâ* and translate it as 'unclean' (NIV) or 'filthy' (ESV). However, others take it from a root meaning either to wander or to shake. Thus, Jerusalem has become either a wanderer (in exile) or the object of head-shaking mockery (NRSV). This would fit with the mocking laughter of the end of v. 7.

mockery as she suffers the exposure inflicted on her as punishment for her infidelity. So painful is this unbearable public torture that the woman herself cannot even bear to look up, but *groans and turns away*, shrinking from the agony of her naked shame (8c). Shifting again from metaphor to reality, the destruction of the city of Jerusalem and the stripping away of every precious thing within it are portrayed as a humiliating exposure of its defenceless nakedness before the surrounding nations. Television footage of bombed and looted cities in modern times gives some inkling of what it means for a city to be 'stripped naked'.

The metaphor of uncleanness caused by promiscuity continues in verse 9a – a promiscuity that had become a headlong rush without thought for the future consequences[13] (as so many prophets had warned). But once again the Poet confuses our emotions and responses. Yes, we have been made aware that this 'woman' is suffering the consequences of her own unfaithfulness and folly. But even knowing that, can we look at her (can we look at her at all?) without pity, without a shudder of horror and a sick stomach, for the agony she now suffers? Are we not also 'astounded' at *her fall* from grace to this hell of disgrace (9b)? Are we not appalled that she is utterly alone with *none to comfort her*? If we cannot condone her sin, are we to condemn it in a way that aligns us with the mocking enemies? Surely not. Surely the Poet is stretching us out in tension between our heads, which tell us to face the facts and consequences of Israel's history, and our hearts, which cry out for pity and mercy on a sobbing woman.

And as the Poet holds us in that tension, we hear the first words of the woman herself – interrupting our narrator and appealing directly over his head and ours to God himself:

Look, Lord, on my affliction,
for the enemy has triumphed.
(9c)

Whose enemy has triumphed? Well, Israel's, of course. But Israel's enemies are God's enemies too – such is the logic of the covenant. Such too was the logic of the marriage metaphor in that culture. A wife exposed to public shame was a shame on her husband, who had failed to either preserve her

---

[13] The text here attributes to Jerusalem the same arrogant disregard for future consequences that Isaiah portrays in his lament over fallen Babylon, Isa. 47:7.

faithfulness or protect her honour. When *the enemy has triumphed*, YHWH God needs to pay attention, for his own honour is being dragged down to the gutter with the woman whose suffering is indirectly the work of God's own hands. That is the terrible dilemma facing God that Ezekiel will wrestle with. In punishing Israel at the hands of her enemies, YHWH has exposed his own name to humiliating ridicule and blasphemy (Ezek. 36:16–36).

The city-woman's plea, scarcely audible we imagine, is not only a plea for God's pity; it implicates God's honour. Two verses later she will repeat the plea: *Look, LORD, and consider, for I am despised* (11c); 'and so are you, because of me' – the unspoken corollary. The woman reaches out to pull God down, forcing him not only to see her pain but also to share her shame, for it is his as well as hers in the eyes of the watching world. Little did she know that God would indeed one day come down, that God himself would suffer nakedness, bearing shame and scoffing rude, despised, rejected, a man of sorrows and acquainted with grief. But we are a long way from that redemptive moment here. Still worse is yet to come.

For what exactly had the enemy done? Verse 10 is, at one level, a simple literal description of Babylon's capture of Jerusalem, during which they carted off all the *treasures* of the city – especially from the temple. There, they had brazenly entered its *sanctuary* to proclaim the victory of the gods of Babylon over whatever god was presumed to make his home there. 'Jackboots have marched in the temple where barbarous hands have besmirched the sacred objects and fouled the holy places where fear and respect should have kept them away.'[14] Such was the way of victorious armies. You conquered the city, you captured its king, you slaughtered its people and you spat on its gods. The shocking trauma of all this is graphically painted in Psalms 74:4–8 and 79:1–4.

But after the lurid imagery of verses 8 and 9, it is very probable that the metaphor of sexual abuse continues here in verse 10. The first phrase reads (Heb.): 'His hand he stretched out, the enemy, over all her precious things.' The image of sexual groping (pawing her) arises, particularly since the hand, *yād*, was also a Hebrew euphemism for the male sexual organ. Then comes, 'She saw nations [pagans] going into her holy place.'

To her horror Jerusalem watched Gentile nations enter her sanctuary. The sexual allusions are clear. The word 'enter' is often used to describe

---

14 Slavitt, *Lamentations*, p. 63.

the act of a man 'entering' a woman in sexual intercourse . . . The image is of [Jerusalem] being raped; indeed the plural 'nations' may suggest that she is being gang-raped.[15]

The multiple rape of women was as much part of the fully intentional horrors of ancient warfare as it still is today. It not only destroys the lives and futures of the women themselves, but also humiliates the men who cannot protect their own women. It symbolizes in the worst possible way the utter triumph of the enemy. In Jerusalem's case, the compounded tragedy is that she who had run after her many lovers among the nations, and their gods, ends up being viciously violated in the very house of the God she had abandoned.

But how could the God who dwelt there allow such a monstrous thing to happen? The Poet cannot hold back from putting his own question before the throne of God. If Lady Zion begs God to look, the Poet nudges God to explain. For the pillaging foreign nations were *those you had forbidden to enter your assembly* (10c). The Deuteronomic ban on foreigners being allowed into the worshipping assembly had applied to Ammonites and Moabites (Deut. 23:3–6). The Poet simply extends the presumed ban to Babylonians (though doubtless Ammonites and Moabites took advantage of the Babylonian victory). So the Poet is caught between the command of God in his law and the sovereignty of God in history. How could God now permit what God himself had prohibited? The question is not put quite like that, but in speaking directly to God (**you** *had forbidden to enter* **your** *assembly*), the Poet leaves it hanging in the air. It is the first of many similar questions that he will hurl aloft in this book.

d. Starved and desperate (1:11)

The Poet shifts from the violence of sexual abuse to the slow torture of starvation, as he brings his first portrait of Jerusalem's suffering to a close. It is a theme that haunts the book,[16] just as the reality of it must have haunted the city itself in those terrible months of siege.

For the third time *their treasures* are mentioned (cf. 7, 10). It could well refer to people giving up their most precious valuables in exchange for any food that was available. Price inflation is a well-known fact of wartime,

---

[15] Parry, p. 54.

[16] See other references to the effects of siege and starvation: 1:19; 2:11; 3:16; 4:10; 5:9–10.

but in sieges and similar extremities hunger will drive people to give any-thing in exchange for food and water. Anything? It is possible that this time the Poet uses *treasures* for the most precious thing in any family – the children. That is how the word is used in Hosea 9:16. If so, what was going on?

Most commentators envisage desperate parents selling their children into slavery for food *to keep themselves alive*. But Adele Berlin challenges that, asking what would be the point of selling children into slavery if there was a limited supply of food to go round anyway. The word *barter* (NIV) is not necessarily what the Hebrew means: it simply says, 'they give their precious things (*sc.* children?) for food, to restore/revive life' (not necessarily *to keep themselves alive*). She suggests that the poorest and weakest people, anticipating their own death by starvation, chose agonizingly to give up their children to others in the hope that they (the children) would be cared for and survive.

> It is not that the parents are making a profit from the sale of their children in order to buy food. Rather the desperate parents, who can no longer feed their children, are forced to give them away for the good of the children . . . The sad irony of our verse is that by giving up their children now, the parents will have no one in the future to provide for them and are, in essence, destroying their families. This terrible choice of keeping one's children with one or giving them up in the hope they would survive often had to be made during the Holocaust.[17]

So we come to the end of the first half of the chapter. The woman herself interrupts again in the last line of verse 11, and this time the Poet lets her continue. The whole second half of the chapter is her voice – with a single comment from the Poet (17). But before we listen, we may marvel at the skill of the Poet's personification of Jerusalem as a woman in distress. The metaphors have tumbled over one another, with ever-increasing raw emotional power.

> Here a kaleidoscope of images turns quickly from a lonely widow, to a degraded princess, to a whore, to a rape victim, to a betrayed lover, to an abandoned wife. The woman betrayed by her lovers is the country

---

[17] Berlin, pp. 56–57.

betrayed by its allies; the mother mourning the loss of her children is the city lamenting the exile of her citizens; the sexual violation of the woman-city is the religious violation of the temple precincts; the sexual sin of immorality is the religious sin of idolatry . . . The poem moves back and forth from the woman to the city in such a way that the figurative and the literal blend together.[18]

2. Zion's cry (1:12–22)

a. The day of God's anger (1:12–17)

Twice she has appealed to God to look at her. But whether God does look or not she cannot tell, for God says nothing. So she turns instead to anyone passing by on the road – even those who were taunting her (cf. Zeph. 2:15). Surely they will take pity on her? Can they not see the incomparable enormity of her suffering? *Is it nothing to you, all you who pass by?* The traditional translation has been hallowed by time and a haunting tenor aria in Handel's *Messiah*.[19] But her words are more mysterious. Literally, she begins, 'Not to you / not for you . . .' If it is a question, it could imply, 'Is this not for you, you who can see what has happened to me?' That is, 'My suffering should be a lesson for you. Learn from it and don't end up where I am.' Or it may be a bitter wish: 'May this not happen to you, whoever you are!'[20]

Her question *Is any suffering like my suffering . . . ?* is rhetorical. She is not asking for a comparative analysis or league tables of suffering. Whatever objective calculus there might be for other devastated cities, for herself Jerusalem can conceive of nothing worse or greater. Her pain is all-consuming.

It is suffering that knows no bounds, beyond comparison with other suffering . . . suffering that defies containment, that blasts away at the imagination, that has no words to express its depth and totality. From her position inside the pain, no one has suffered as much as she because there is no way she could imagine more suffering.[21]

---

18 Berlin, pp. 47–48.
19 'Behold, and see if there be any sorrow.'
20 Parry, p. 56.
21 O'Connor, p. 26.

But what makes her words so poignant is her awareness of where all this suffering has come from. It is from the hand of the same God to whom she has appealed twice already (9c, 11c). It is as though she now at last, in the midst of incomparable pain and with infinite effort, accepts in verse 12c what the Poet has already pointed out in verses 5b and 8a. Her sin has finally brought down upon her consequences that God had said would surely follow.

The day God had threatened had finally come, *the day of his fierce anger*. Undoubtedly this is an echo of many passages in the prophets that had spoken ominously of 'the day of the LORD'. Amos was probably the first to turn an expression that originally would have signified the day of God's deliverance of Israel through victory over their enemies into a threat of judgment ahead. After him, it was used by the pre-exilic prophets predominantly in that negative sense: *Dies irae*, the day of God's wrath (Amos 5:18–20; 8:8–14; Isa. 2:12–21; Joel 1:15; 2:1–11; Zeph. 1:7–18). For Jerusalem, that day came in 587 BC, when the walls were breached, the Babylonian army swarmed into the city, and the world collapsed around her.

What was it like to live through that terrible day? The city-woman describes it in verses 13–15 in vivid pictures all drawn from the world of siege warfare. Once again, the literal and metaphorical meanings of words blend together. Besieged cities were attacked with fire, and often burnt when the siege was successful (13a). Nets were used to capture fugitives, or to pen in prisoners (13b). Prisoners were often yoked together by the neck (14). Defeated soldiers were trampled, alive or dead (15).

But the city-woman's choice of words is specific and sharp, like a jabbing finger. She could have spoken in the first person: '*I* or *we* were burned, caught, yoked, trampled.' Or she could have used the plural, referring to the Babylonians: '*They* attacked us with fire, caught us in nets, chained us together . . .' But the verbs are all relentlessly singular. Who did all these things? *He* did! *He, the* LORD of verse 12c. *He sent fire . . . He spread a net . . . his hands* wove the yoke . . . *He has given me into the hands . . . He has summoned an army . . . the Lord has trampled . . .* Behind the Babylonians stood the God of Israel *in the day of his fierce anger*.

This is why I weep (16).

And no wonder, we think. The emotional turmoil of awareness, acceptance, questions and lament swirls through her tears. She has accepted that her sins have brought God's anger, but anger and destruction on *this* scale?

On the other hand, the yoke of defeated slavery that God had now placed on her neck was constructed from her own sins (14) – a very powerful way of saying that God's judgment on sinful Israel was not a kind of extraneous punishment like a whipping, a fine or imprisonment, but was actually the rebound of her own evil folly. Evil sown produces evil reaped. Judah was warned repeatedly – right up to the last minute by Jeremiah – that rebellion against Babylon would produce horrendous levels of death and destruction, but that they could avoid the worst of those consequences by surrendering rather than persisting in rebellion. But they chose rebellion and paid the price. Their own politics produced their punishment, the sword of Babylon wielding the judgment of God.

So she accepts what the prophets (especially Jeremiah) had said – that Babylon was merely the tool of God's sovereignty.[22] But did that justify the horrendous violence of Babylon's war machine? (She will come back to that question with vehemence at the end of the chapter.) And above all, how had the God who was supposed to be *inside* Jerusalem defending it become the God *outside* the city leading the triumphant pagan armies into it for their orgy of rampage, rape and desecration? The irony of that is somewhat hidden by the English translation of verse 15a: *The Lord has rejected all the warriors in my midst.* Actually, the words 'in my midst' go with 'the Lord', not the warriors. The subject comes at the end of the sentence. In Hebrew the line reads: 'He has rejected (i.e. he despises as worthless, hardly worth fighting) all my warriors, the Lord in the midst of me.' The last phrase clearly echoes the great affirmation of Psalm 46:5, 'God is in the midst of her, she shall not fall' (my translation). That psalm celebrates the security of the city of God in the face of all disasters, enemies and wars. That was one of the songs of Zion they would not be singing by the rivers of Babylon, then (Ps. 137). God the defender had become God the attacker.[23] With enemies like that, no friend could have helped her anyway (7b, 16b). When *those I cannot withstand* (14) include God himself, despair seems total.

Lady Zion pauses for breath amidst her overflowing *tears*. Thoughts of her *destitute children* (16c) leave her with nothing but a sobbing gesture, which the Poet sees and interprets on her behalf (17). Verse 17 is a brief

---

[22] In Jer. 27, he even affirmed that YHWH regarded Nebuchadnezzar as 'my servant' – i.e. the one who was carrying out the will of God at that moment in history.

[23] Ezekiel's acted mimes in which he portrayed, in his own person, God besieging and attacking his own city from outside, made the same point (Ezek. 4 – 5).

word in the third person before the city-woman comes back with her second speech (18–22).

Zion stretches out her hands – like a beggar or suppliant in silent appeal. The Poet sees her gesture but nobody else does. Nobody sees or cares (17a). Echoing Zion's own lament (16b), and for the fourth time in the chapter, we are told *there is no one to comfort her*. And that is bad enough, but what makes it worse is the reason the Poet now adds. *The Lord has decreed for Jacob that his neighbours become his foes* (17b). Now we know why none of the surrounding nations came to Judah's aid, before, during or after the siege. At one level, simply international politics at its most vicious and selfish. But behind even that lies the sovereign decree of Israel's God. Israel must bear her judgment alone. Other nations wouldn't even touch her, let alone help her (17c).[24]

b. The day of God's justice (1:18–22)

Lady Zion finds her voice again. A controlled and chastened voice at first (18), but quickly changing tone to lament her lonely suffering (19–21b), then rising with anger (21c–22b), before finally sinking back to feeble groaning once more (22c). Since God had apparently not responded to her previous appeals, she now addresses the nations – *all you peoples* (18b). But they are spectators in the drama (and not even very attentive ones). The dialogue she longs for, like Job, is with God himself. And so, undaunted by his silence, she turns yet again to plead with God to look at her (20). This woman is desperate for God's attention, and even more for God's justice.

Justice is actually where she starts – the justice of God's dealings with her. Verse 18 is her clearest confession of the truth about God and the truth about herself. The opening line is simple and emphatic:

> 'Righteous is he, YHWH; for against his mouth (word) did I rebel.' She
> confesses openly her guilt to the peoples around, and declares thereby that
> it is not the might of the enemy that has prevailed but the justice of God.[25]

---

[24] Once again the metaphor of ritual uncleanness needs careful interpretation. *An unclean thing* translates *niddâ*, which, as we saw earlier, refers to a menstruating woman. However, there is no implication that a menstruating woman is, for that reason, in any sense sinful or immoral. It is merely that she should not participate for a week in the worshipping assemblies, and her husband should refrain from intercourse (Lev. 18:19; a sensitive consideration in any case). The point of the metaphor in v. 17c is simply that other nations would stay away from Israel as an Israelite husband would avoid contact with his menstrual wife.

[25] Re'emi, pp. 89–90.

Her words would later be echoed by Ezra and Nehemiah in their prayers of confession of the sins of Israel going back generations (Ezra 9:13–15; Neh. 9:33). Going back, in fact, as far as the generation of the exodus. For the word *I rebelled* is the verb *mārâ* which figured prominently in the grumbling rebellions of the Israelites in the wilderness (Num. 20:10, 24; 27:14; Deut. 1:26, 43; 9:7, 23–24). 'If such an allusion is intended, we may see that God's people have not changed at all since the days of the exodus and rebel now as they did then.'[26] That, indeed, had been the constant message of the prophets, against whose words they had continued to rebel right up to the last weeks before the fall of Jerusalem – and even after it.

So Lady Zion confesses God's moral justice and her own sinful rebellion (18). And that is a key moment in the theology of the whole book. There will be times in the coming chapters when we may find it hard to remember that she actually said it. But even as she affirms the truth in that moment of clear self-awareness, her suffering drives her back into raw self-pity. 'Even as Jerusalem declares her guilt from her own mouth, she still seeks sympathy from others.'[27] Her appeal to the nations to *listen* to her and *look* on her suffering (18b) may have an element of warning ('Look what has happened to me. Do not rebel against God as I did'). But even if that is part of her thinking, it is quickly swallowed up in the wrenching pain of lost children (18c), false friends[28] (19a), and people starving to death while searching for food (19b–c).

Nevertheless, she *has* said it: *The Lord is righteous.* And in that foundational affirmation of Old Testament faith, she has said more than she probably meant in the immediate circumstances. What she means here is that God has acted justly within the terms of the covenant; God is justified in finally bringing upon her (after centuries of warning) the consequences of persistent rebellion against her covenant Lord – as justified as any king would be in acting against rebellious subjects. In the current situation, God is in the right and she is the convicted rebel, justly punished.

But if her tortured mind could only recall the old stories of her people, or any snatches of the Psalms, then surely she would remember that the

---

[26] Parry, p. 62.

[27] Berlin, p. 59.

[28] The word *my allies* (19) is the same as in v. 2 – her *lovers*. Once again we find the seemingly unconscious irony that Jerusalem who had so betrayed her husband YHWH finds it shocking that her lovers have now betrayed her. But that is what the prophets had warned all along: if you trust in these other nations, you will be bitterly disappointed. And she was.

righteousness of God was the constant foundation for Israel's hope and prayer for deliverance. And it would be again. The God whose righteousness had sent her into exile would, in his righteousness, bring her back. The God of Israel is as righteous in salvation as in judgment. And for that reason not only could Lady Zion turn back to him eventually, but ultimately so could all the nations to whom she so forlornly appeals.

> There is no God apart from me,
>> a righteous God and a Saviour . . .
> Turn to me and be saved,
>> all you ends of the earth;
>> for I am God, and there is no other.
> (Isa. 45:21–22; my italics)

But such hope is far from her thinking in the day of disaster. Her thoughts are in turmoil (20a), tormented by the moral and spiritual pain of her guilt (20b), by the physical pain of death and destruction (20c), and by the emotional pain of the obscene rejoicing of her enemies at her downfall (21a–b).

And that last awareness – that her enemies are actually gloating with joy at the suffering God's judgment has brought her – sparks a final burst of energy. She prays for another *day – the day you have announced* (21c).[29] What day was that? Almost certainly this is the original sense of the 'day of the Lord', the day when he would judge and destroy his enemies. The concept has deep roots in Israel's traditions. It goes back to the Song of Moses in Deuteronomy 32.

Anticipating Israel's future story, Deuteronomy 32 portrays Israel's unfaithfulness, idolatry and corruption. It warns Israel (as the covenant curses had done in Deut. 28) that God will bring against them enemy nations – foreigners whom they despised – who will batter Israel almost to the point of total extinction (Deut. 32:21–26). But, in a crucial turning point in the chapter, God realizes that those enemies would take credit for their victory and taunt YHWH and his people (32:27). God could not

---

[29] The NIV, like most other translations, takes the whole of 21c as a prayer, *May you bring the day you have announced*, assuming that the 'day' in question means the day when God would judge Israel's enemies. However, some (e.g. ESV) take the words as a simple statement, 'You have brought the day you announced.' This links it to the preceding words, 'You have done it.' That is, God's judgment on Jerusalem was what God had warned them about well beforehand. Now God had done it, he had brought that day. Either fits the context, but the former and more common translation is probably correct.

tolerate that, and so the enemies themselves will become the target of his anger. The God who has brought judgment on his own people through other nations will in turn judge those nations also.

It is mine to avenge; I will repay.
In due time their foot will slip;
their day of disaster is near
and their doom rushes upon them.[30]

That is the day Jerusalem now wants to see. 'She seems to have understood that the instrument God uses against her today will not escape his judgment tomorrow (Jer. 51:24, 35–37).'[31]

At one level, it is an all-too-realistic and understandable reaction to the ghastly carnage that her enemies had inflicted on her. Reeling under such treatment, she cries out for some compensating suffering to be meted out to them, as does the chilling close of Psalm 137, birthed in the same cauldron of pain. Let Zion's fate become theirs too: *so that they may become like me* (21c). We may not like the sentiment, but we can understand it.

Two things prevent us, however, from dismissing these fierce closing lines of the city-woman's lament as a crude lust for vengeance. First, she is calling on God to do what God said he would do. Let him keep his word. The day she wants is the day God had announced long ago.[32] It was a core element of Israel's faith (and part of New Testament faith too, we might add), attested in multiple scriptures, that YHWH is the God who will judge and ultimately destroy the wicked. Could anything more wicked be conceived than what Babylon had done to Jerusalem? Even if it was serving the purpose of God's judgment, it was still an act of wanton bloody violence. Would not then the Judge of all the earth do justice and take action against them too?

Second, Jerusalem has not lost sight of her own guilt. Her demand is not 'God, slap them down in your anger, and let me off the hook.' This is not an exercise in self-justification or odious comparison ('Why should I suffer

---

[30] Deut. 32:35 (my italics; cf. 41–42). The words 'their' and 'them' in the text refer to the enemies of Israel, falling under the judgment of God.

[31] Coulibaly, pp. 951–958.

[32] And repeated through the prophets – e.g. Isa. 13:13, using exactly the same phrase as in 12c ('day of [the Lord's] fierce anger'), against Babylon itself.

when they are even worse than me?'). Verse 22a–b is a carefully balanced chiasm:

> Let all *their* evil come before you;
>> deal with *them*
>> according as you have dealt with *me*
> on account of all *my* rebellion.
> (My translation)

All Jerusalem asks is for God to be fair.

> Justice demands that YHWH deal with the enemies according to their deeds, just as he dealt with Jerusalem according to her deeds . . . Notice that there is no attempt to plead her innocence. Rather she calls for God to notice *all* evils and not merely *her* evils.[33]

She is not complaining that God's treatment of *her* is not fair, but that it is not fair if others who are equally wicked are not dealt with in the same way. Let God judge them too!

We will hear this cry for justice in even harsher language at the end of chapter 3, and will consider it further there. For now, the city-woman, Lady Zion, has mustered all she can say. The effort of giving voice to her suffering, and appealing for God, or anyone, to pay attention to her cries, has exhausted her. She sinks back, groaning and fainting, into the suffering solitude in which we first found her (22c).

Reflections

1. How do you see the interplay between judgment on Lady Zion for her acknowledged sin, and pity for her in her suffering? Does that affect the way we think about 'bad people', convicted criminals, or those who suffer the effects of their own folly? Is there a place for sympathy along with condemnation?

2. 'She can deny neither her failure nor her neediness. Her neediness is something that only God can fully grasp and only God can fully heal. One function of lamentation is to give voice to her failures, so

---

[33] Parry, p. 65 (italics original).

that God will recognize in her voice an indication of confession and an appeal for mercy.'[34] How do you see the balance between *failure* and *need*? And how does that affect how we respond?

3. In what sense, if any, does Christ speak in this chapter?

---

[34] Dearman, p. 445.

Lamentations 2:1–22

2. In the day of God's anger

Jerusalem, the city-woman, may have sunk into sobbing silence (1:22c), but the Poet has plenty of voice left. Once more he cries out *'êkâ!* and launches into a passionately graphic account of the utter demolition of the city at the hands of the Babylonians. If he was an eyewitness (and there is every indication from the detail of his observation that he was),[1] then that was indeed who he saw doing it – the ruthless battalions and engines of Babylon's victorious armed forces. But they, the human enemies, are not even mentioned until verse 16. The real enemy whose onslaught had reduced Jerusalem to rubble was the Lord God himself. The first eight verses pound our ears with a relentless salvo of twenty-eight verbs portraying destruction on a blockbuster scale, and every one has God as the subject. 'He' is repeated in almost every line. And after the crushing bombardment, nothing is left but deathly 'silence' in the dust (10).

The chapter has a similar structure to chapter 1. The Poet begins with his objective account of what he has seen (1–10). Then comes a first-person section – but this time it is not the city-woman who speaks (as happens at 1:12). She does not have the strength to say anything until urged and begged by the Poet himself, and even then she only manages the last three verses (20–22). Rather, it is the Poet who breaks into first-person speech at verse 11, unable to hold back the emotional storm that breaks within him. He weeps in sympathy with the city-woman, Lady Zion, and speaks directly to her in a futile (but noble) attempt to comfort her (13). So moved

---

[1] And if, as I assume, the Poet of ch. 3 is the same person who speaks here in ch. 2, then the eyewitness claim is explicit (3:1).

is the Poet by the plight of the children (11c–12) that he begs Lady Zion to cry out to God on their behalf, if not her own (18–19). Finally, she responds to his urgent exhortation and turns yet again to the Lord – the one who has attacked her so brutally! – and appeals to him to 'look' at her and 'consider' (20–22). Can even God bear to contemplate the consequences of his own actions? At the end of the day, the day of his anger, will he too be always and only 'my enemy' (22c)?

So the structure of the chapter is straightforward:

- 1–10: The Poet describes what God has done to Jerusalem.
- 11–19: The Poet expresses his own pain, seeks to comfort Jerusalem, and urges her to cry out to God, her only hope.
- 20–22: Lady Zion speaks, asking God once more to 'Look . . . and consider'.

Less straightforward, however, is how we should interpret the mood of this chapter. At one level, it is obvious. As in chapter 1, we are confronted with immense suffering caused by the cataclysmic destruction not only of a city, but also of the whole social, political and religious community within it, along with all their systems and symbols of peoplehood. The disaster engulfs every building and everybody, men and women, old and young, from respected elders to suckling infants. So: shock, grief, agony, numbed silence, horror, revulsion, tears in abundance, searing questions – all of these we can see and hear.

And anger too? Certainly the anger of God. That envelops the chapter with 'cloud' and 'terrors on every side' (1, 22). But is anger also being expressed by the Poet and the city-woman? Human anger *at* God? It is hard to read through verses 1–10 without sensing the Poet's increasing note of protest at the devastation he has witnessed.[2] And it is even harder to resist that impression when he makes it personal in 3:1–17 as the devastation he has experienced. But then, there is good precedent in the Old Testament for protesting to God in the midst of suffering and evil. Job does it; Jeremiah does it; and many of the psalms do it. It is a standard part of the genre of lament to cry out to God: 'God, this suffering is

---

[2] It is a 'sensing'. 'God is angry with Israel, and, from the tone in which that anger is described, we sense that the poet is angry with God' (Berlin, p. 67). The poet never explicitly speaks of himself being angry, but rather of his own pain and grief (11). Yet the sheer power and violence of his language seem to express a latent anger and protest at what he describes.

intolerable! This evil is an atrocious, violent offence against your whole created order! Why do you allow it? Why do you inflict it?' God has broad enough shoulders to cry on and a big enough chest to beat against. God even provides words in his Scriptures to permit us, indeed to encourage us, to do so. It is *right* to cry out and protest about evil – and whatever other theological dimensions we must apply to the fall of Jerusalem in 587 BC, it did embody an orgy of evil. So when we find acute human anger here, it is neither surprising nor sinful in itself.

And accusation? Is the Poet *accusing* God of going too far? Are the combined voices of the Poet and the city-woman hauling God into court, hurling at him the charge of being a brutal aggressor, an enraged abuser, a warmonger guilty of crimes against humanity? Some commentators read the chapter in that 'mood'. The Poet in chapter 2 has been converted, as it were, from his judgmental stance in chapter 1, in which he blamed Lady Zion for her own suffering ('blaming the victim' being a well-known tendency), to become her sympathetic companion. He enters into her suffering and is appalled by the horror of what God has done to her. He becomes her advocate *against* God. God is now the one under judgment, not her.

That is the line taken by Kathleen O'Connor in her powerful (and often deeply moving) commentary. Here is how she reads this chapter:

> While the narrator depicts the assault on land and people, he is simultaneously charging God with infidelity, lack of integrity, and loss of self-control. God's actions are vicious . . . God is mad, out of control, swirling about in unbridled destruction . . . More shocking still is the narrator's accusation that God acted out of calculated cruelty. YHWH 'planned' to destroy . . . (2:8) . . . the attack on the city was not merely an accidental result of momentary passion, but planned and decided with malice and forethought . . . [Zion's] guilt fades from poetic concern, and the narrator's charges are against God alone . . . He forgets her guilt and his accusations in chapter 1 and turns furiously against the divine attacker.[3]

It seems to me, however, that one can sustain that kind of reading (which surely involves a lot of interpretive eisegesis from a modern

---

3 O'Connor, pp. 33–34. See the discussion of this issue also in the Introduction section 2c, pp. 17–19.

perspective) only by ignoring at least two major considerations. One is the agreement throughout the whole book, between the Poet and Lady Zion, that God's actions were in direct response to Jerusalem's persistent rebellion, that the 'plan' had been 'announced' as a warning long before (so that it could have been averted), and that, far from his being deliberately malicious, vicious or out of control, it gave God no pleasure whatsoever to witness what the human agents of his judgment did (3:33). The other thing that O'Connor seems to give very little attention to at all is the depth of canonical resonances in the chapter. As we shall see, the whole picture reflects the covenant curses of Leviticus 26 and Deuteronomy 27 – 28. Israel had been warned from the very beginning of their journey with God that the consequences of persistent covenant rebellion would be extreme, because they would be inflicted by the hands of cruel, fallen, implacable human beings. Babylonians will do what Babylonians will do. And has O'Connor not read Jeremiah? For forty years he had painted in advance and in detail the very scenes described in this chapter (to his own weeping agony in doing so) – for the precise purpose of urging Judah to take a different path and avoid such a fate. The point is: Lamentations 2 *need not have happened*. But when it did, it was nothing other than 'the day' (1:12, 21) that God had warned about at least since the prophet Amos, nearly two hundred years earlier.

So, to be sure, there is reeling shock and gut-wrenching pain. There are tones of angry protest and lament at the excessive suffering, especially of innocent children. There are questions to be asked – and asked of God himself. There is a massive sense of disorientation and desperation, and a strong suspicion of disproportionality. But in the context of the whole book and its canonical framework, there is no accusation (in the sense of guilt and blame), in my view, that God's action in the destruction of Jerusalem was unjustified – an act of inexplicable wanton malice. The combination of Israel's own religious unfaithfulness, moral corruption and political folly – unrepented and undeterred by multiple warnings – made it inevitable. God said it would happen, and here is what happened when it did.

> The drumbeat of what God has done is not so much a series of accusations as it is a thorough statement of fact . . . From start to finish the poem charts what it means to experience God's direct, purposeful, unstinting judgment. It also moves readers from

description (2:1–10), to concern and counsel (2:11–19), to direct address to God (2:20–22).[4]

1. The city torn down to the ground (2:1–10)

Down, down, down, down. This whole first part of the poem ruthlessly drags everything down towards the ground: the city, the fortifications, the princes, the temple, the walls, the gates, the people. It begins with the temple being spiritually hurled down *from heaven to earth* (1) and ends with *elders* and *young women* sitting on the ground, covered in dust, heads *bowed . . . to the ground* (10). God the demolisher.

a. No mercy (2:1–5)

The phrase that God acted *without pity* (2; lit. 'he did not have compassion'), which comes three times in the chapter (2, 17, 21), is uncomfortable, and might seem to reinforce the picture of God as a brutal aggressor that we were disputing a moment ago. Surely yhwh defined himself as the God who *does* have compassion, who *does* show mercy (Exod. 34:6)? Indeed so, but then what else had God been doing for the past centuries when Israel's sin had gone on accumulating generation after generation? Joel promised that God would '[take] pity [same verb] on his people', on the foundation of their sincere repentance (Joel 2:12–18). But that repentance had never been truly forthcoming. The Chronicler even interpreted the fact that God had sent many prophets to warn the people as being in itself an act of God's compassion designed to avert the catastrophe ahead.

> The Lord, the God of their ancestors, sent word to them through his messengers again and again, *because he had pity on his people and on his dwelling-place.* But they mocked God's messengers, despised his words and scoffed at his prophets until the wrath of the Lord was aroused against his people and there was no remedy. He brought up against them the king of the Babylonians, who killed their young men with the sword in the sanctuary, and did not spare young men or young women, the elderly or the infirm. God gave them all into the hands of Nebuchadnezzar.[5]

---

[4] House, pp. 372, 375.

[5] 2 Chr. 36:15–17 (my italics; and the same verb as in Lam. 2:2).

Exactly what Lamentations 2 portrays.

> For God to not have mercy means that the time for sending warning
> prophets has ended. It may also indicate that God's warning mercy has
> ceased because no repentance like that found in Joel 2:1–18 has occurred.
> Israel has enjoyed God's mercy for centuries but does not do so at this
> point in time.[6]

Stepping back to the start of the chapter, what exactly had God done to
Zion? Most translations read the opening verb to mean that he had *covered*
it with the dark *cloud of his anger*. That would certainly fit what follows.
It could mean the dark thunderclouds that were associated with God's
presence (Pss 68:4; 97:2; 104:3), and especially with the day of the Lord
(Joel 2:2; Zeph. 1:15), or simply that the city was cut off from God's face
and favour by a separating cloud. In either case, it would be in stark
contrast to the cloud that symbolized the guiding and protecting presence
of God in the wilderness, or the cloud of his glory that filled the tabernacle
and temple (Exod. 13:21–22; 40:34–38; 1 Kgs 8:10–11). But some scholars
read the verb as *yāʿîb* – the verbal form of *tôʿēbâ*, 'abomination' – and
translate, 'God has made Zion loathsome; turned it into an abomination'.[7]
That too fits the context well, since God's actions against the city in the
searing verses that follow match the kind of destruction associated with
God's curse, illustrated in the classic overthrow of Sodom and Gomorrah
(cf. Deut. 29:23).

The first reference to the 'down to the ground' motif is the most graphic
and the farthest distance – *from heaven to earth*. God had *hurled down the
splendour of Israel*. That could refer to everything that was beautiful and
glorious about Israel, but in the context it almost certainly refers to the
temple in particular. The mention of *his footstool* in the last line strongly
suggests that. And although the next few verses speak about other buildings
(and we get to the temple more unambiguously in vv. 6–7), we recall that
Zion was above all the place of the worship of yhwh. So the temple was the
most important building in the city and gets mentioned first.

But in what sense was the temple *hurled down . . . from heaven to earth*?
In Israel (as in other cultures at that time) a temple was where heaven and

---

6 House, p. 377.
7 Berlin, pp. 67–68.

earth met. The temple was the earthly address, so to speak, of gods who lived in the heavens. Now in Israel's case, they knew that YHWH their God did not literally live in the temple. Solomon, who built the temple, was well aware that the living God of all creation would 'overflow' the heavens and certainly could not be contained in a small building on earth – however splendid in itself (1 Kgs 8:27–30). Nevertheless, it was where God had promised to place his name. And when God met with his people in their worship and sacrifices at that place, or when God heard their prayers offered in, or towards, the temple, there was a sense in which heaven and earth came together. The temple was a microcosm – literally, a 'tiny cosmos' – of the whole creation ('heaven and earth'), which was the true dwelling-place of God.[8] In that sense, the temple on earth reflected the 'temple' of God's perfect presence in heaven (a concept that the writer to the Hebrews expands in some detail).

So in destroying the temple, God has cut off the link between heaven and earth – hurling it down to earth. It is a shattering picture of a broken relationship.

The rest of this section (2–5) catalogues the destruction of the country and its defences. When an enemy army invaded, the villages and fortifications in the surrounding countryside would be demolished first before they turned their attention to the main city. That's what verse 2 describes (notice the use of *Judah*, not just Jerusalem). The Babylonians had *swallowed up* the rest of the kingdom (tiny as it was). *Every horn* (3a) is a metaphor for strong men in general and military strength especially (just as a bull or stag uses its horns as a weapon of defence or attack; e.g. Pss 75:10; 89:17, 24; 112:9; 132:17). But of course, Israel's ultimate defender was God himself, whose right hand had delivered them from Egypt centuries before and protected them ever since. No longer. That divine *right hand* that would once have driven back the enemy has been *withdrawn* (3b). And the divine *fire* that would have consumed their enemies is now consuming Israel itself (3c).

In the Exodus narratives fire, like cloud, is a symbol of God's presence with Israel for blessing (e.g. Exod. 13:21–22). God's right hand is also very

---

[8] Isa. 66:1–2 makes the point: heaven was God's throne, the earth his footstool. God sits, as it were, with his throne in heaven and his footstool on earth – represented by the temple. The Jerusalem temple, then, was not a house within which 'the whole of God' lived. It was merely a footstool for the creator of the whole universe. Creation as a whole is his temple.

much in evidence in those narratives, operating on Israel's behalf (Exod. 15:6, 12). Now his right hand is no longer with them, and the fire, like the cloud, symbolizes only his wrath. Truly God has turned against them![9]

God has not just withdrawn, or turned against them, he has now actively become the *enemy* of Israel. This terrifying reality is doubly affirmed in verses 4 and 5, and becomes personal when Lady Zion speaks of 'my enemy' in verse 22. The whole idea of YHWH the God of Israel becoming the enemy of Israel seems surprising and outrageous. But it was exactly what had been described in the threats that were implicit in the covenant relationship. The historical event that Lamentations portrays in graphic horror (Jerusalem being attacked and ravaged by enemies as the action of God in judgment) was the final outworking of the covenant curses that had stood as warnings in the Law and Prophets for centuries (Lev. 26:23–34; Deut. 28:49–52).

God's right hand, once their sure defence, is now the hand of an enemy archer, taking aim with his bow and arrows, in a kind of mass shooting of *all who were pleasing to the eye* (4b). The phrase speaks of those who are precious and loved.[10] Doubtless they were precious to their own families in the stricken city, but the text does not specify *whose* eye, and it is not impossible that it implies that God is striking down those who were precious in his own eyes. Those eyes of God wept tears in the tears of Jeremiah (Jer. 9:9–11; 10:17–25), and it may even be that it is the voice of God speaking through the tears that begin in verse 11. The *mourning and lamentation* that *he has multiplied* (5) included God's own.

b. No worship (2:6–7)

The Poet returns to the burnt-out rubble of the temple and ponders its full significance. The word *his dwelling* means a 'hut' or temporary tent, such as was used by Israelites in the Feast of Tabernacles (Succoth). It was a less than glorious word for the temple, suggesting its transience. God had smashed it down as easily as one might wreck a garden shed.[11] The fact

---

[9] Provan, p. 62.

[10] The most touching use of the phrase is when God describes Ezekiel's young wife in that way, as 'the delight of your eyes' – the day before she was snatched from him in death (Ezek. 24:15–18).

[11] That seems to be the probable significance of the words *like a garden*. Cf. Isa. 1:8, where the same image is used for Jerusalem as a whole – like a shack built in a field to give shelter to the person keeping watch over the crop. Job 27:18 uses a variant of the same word to describe the house of a wicked person as nothing more than 'a hut made by a watchman'.

that the tent in the wilderness had been replaced by an impressive structure of stone and cedar did not make it any more indestructible than the temporary dwelling-place that God had destroyed at Shiloh centuries earlier – as Jeremiah had so offensively pointed out in the courts of the temple itself (Jer. 7:12–14; 26:4–16).[12]

But it was not just the loss of a beautiful building that caused such pain and loss. The temple was the *place of meeting*, where Israel came to worship YHWH in *her appointed festivals and her Sabbaths*.[13] But now all that is gone, forgotten (6b). The temple was also the place of sacrifice, where people came to benefit from the ministry of priests in offering thanksgiving and receiving cleansing and atonement. But now God *has rejected his altar*. The sacrifices also are gone (7a). Without worship in the temple and the work of the priests at the altar – all that the sacrificial system represented within Israel's relationship with God – how could that relationship survive? The language is viciously strong: God has *spurned . . . rejected . . . abandoned* (6c–7a). But it is also reciprocal. For Israel had done the same! *Israel* had rejected and abandoned their God repeatedly and systematically for generations – from the first generation out of Egypt in fact (Num. 14:23; Hos. 8:1–3; Jer. 2:13, 19; 23:17; Ps. 107:11). Indeed, when Jeremiah records some prayers of the people, seeming to plead with God *not* to spurn them in this way, he is starkly reminded of the fact that *it was the people who had consistently rejected God* and would face the consequences eventually (Jer. 14:8–9, 19; 15:6–7; 16:10–13). Those consequences have now happened. Jeremiah also pointed the way to a hope beyond rejection (Jer. 33:23–26), but that is not what comes to the Poet's mind as he sees Israel's enemies holding their jubilant anti-festival in the ruins of the temple they had destroyed (7c). The shuddering horrendous obscenity of that can be felt if you pause to read Psalms 74 and 79. The first halves of those psalms are like background scenery to this part of Lamentations.

Next to the temple was the king's palace, and that too had been razed by the enemy (7b). God had *spurned both king and priest* (6c), the political and religious hierarchy of the nation.

> The holy city of Jerusalem, the temple God had established for his
> worship, the divinely-appointed festivals and Sabbaths, the Davidic king

---

[12] Jeremiah was very nearly put to death for this prediction. Jesus would seal his own death sentence by predicting the same thing in his own day. Both of them were proved right, however, in 587 BC and in AD 70.

[13] The great annual festivals are described in Deut. 16.

God had set in place, the Levitical priests the Lord commanded to serve him – all rejected! This was the end of the world.[14]

c. No wall (2:8–9a)

The Poet's gaze moves outwards from the temple and palace in the centre of the city to the *wall* that surrounded it. That had been torn down just as systematically as it had been built – using the tools of construction as tools of destruction (8b). And along with the walls, all the *ramparts, gates* and *bars* – all the structures of fortification and systems of defence – have *wasted away . . . sunk into the ground . . .* are *broken and destroyed.* Again, the language is vivid and forceful. This is a shattered city. God the demolisher is fulfilling the word of Jeremiah 1:10 to the utmost.

But it is not just that God is fulfilling his word, he is actually carrying out his plan. *The LORD determined . . .* and *The LORD has done what he planned* (8, 17). The terrible destruction of Jerusalem was not an act of random violence inflicted on unsuspecting people. It was not God raging out of control. It was planned.

Now that might seem to make it even worse. Kathleen O'Connor sees this verse as 'more shocking still . . . God had acted out of calculated cruelty . . . with malice and forethought'.[15] But that is to ignore the way the whole concept of God's 'plan' had been outlined in the book of Jeremiah. This was not some secret divine machination, an evil cosmic conspiracy, hidden from view until it burst forth in awesome devastation. On the contrary, God had spoken clearly in advance about the judgment he was planning, precisely so that the people could take action to avert it if they chose to. It was not an irreversible plan. It was not a predetermined fate that nothing could change. It was a *conditional* plan, and if conditions had changed, so would the plan.

That is the clear message of Jeremiah 18. Just as the potter could declare an intention, but then change his plans and do something different in response to some factor in the clay, so God could declare his plans, but also change them in response to how his people reacted.[16] Accordingly, God gives Judah due warning, and invites them to respond appropriately.

---

14 Parry, p. 77.

15 O'Connor, p. 35.

16 This has been appropriately described as God's 'responsive sovereignty'. See my broader discussion of the profound theology of Jer. 18 in *The Message of Jeremiah* (London: Inter-Varsity Press, 2023), pp. 204–215.

> Now therefore say to the people of Judah and those living in Jerusalem,
> 'This is what the Lord says: look! I am preparing a disaster for you and
> devising a plan against you. So turn from your evil ways, each one of you,
> and reform your ways and your actions.'

But that is precisely what they would not do.

> But they will reply, 'It's no use. We will continue with our own plans
> [same word]; we will all follow the stubbornness of our evil hearts.'
> (Jer. 18:11–12)

Well, says God, if that is *your* plan (to refuse to repent and carry on as
before), then *my* plan will have to stand. You leave me no other option. And
in the end, only one plan would win the day (Jer. 19:7–13). And that was the
plan now being carried out.

> For those who heard Jeremiah's living voice, God's message from the
> potter's shop comes to this:

> I offered you every chance to bring about a different future from
> the one that is staring you in the face. I have been patient and open,
> willing to adjust my plans to your choices, like a potter working with
> changeable clay. Even now for the last time I warn you of what lies
> ahead and urge you to take the necessary steps to avert it. If you
> will not, then the full force of my judgment will fall upon you, as
> Jeremiah has predicted for years. But you will never be able to say
> I didn't warn you, or that there was no alternative. There was, and
> you refused it.[17]

Jeremiah would later tell those who had suffered and survived the
catastrophe that God had another plan, expressed as a promise that has
reassured believers ever since (Jer. 29:11).[18] But standing in the ruins of
Jerusalem, the Poet's horizon does not stretch that far . . . yet.

---

[17] Wright, *Jeremiah*, p. 209.

[18] In the circumstances, it is a very surprising plan indeed. This wonderful promise is often quoted with
no awareness of its context: it was given to people under God's judgment, and with the expected response
of a whole-hearted seeking God in repentance.

d. No word (2:9b–10)

So far the Poet's gaze has been absorbed mainly with the physical structures of Jerusalem (apart from the mention of 'both king and priest' in v. 6) – the temple, the palaces, the walls and fortifications. Now he turns to the people, starting at the top (*her king and her princes,* 9b), who have been carried off into exile, and ending with the *young women* (10c), who are left behind, sagging in the dust of the abandoned streets.

What can be said in such desperate circumstances? What might we hope to hear from anyone who can speak a word of comfort, or a word of explanation from the God who is inflicting such pain? When you need a word from God, you would turn to those who were custodians of that word: priests, who could teach and interpret *the law*; *prophets,* who would bring a more direct word from the visions God gave them; and *elders,* who had the wisdom and experience to provide advice and guidance for the rest of the people. But all three groups of leaders have fallen silent in the teeth of such overwhelming disaster. And their silence is the silence of God himself. After all, God had been speaking through the law and the prophets for generations to ears that would not listen. Now they would listen in vain for any word from God at all.

Once again, there seems to be an echo here of Jeremiah 18. When Jeremiah's enemies plotted to get rid of him, they justified their intentions to themselves with the thought that 'the teaching of the law by the priest will not cease, nor will counsel from the wise, nor the word from the prophets' (Jer. 18:18). This indicates that there were at least three distinct 'professional' groups in Israel at the time with recognized public authority in what they might teach, preach or advise: namely priests, prophets and wise men and women. The sad fact was, however, that all three had corrupted their 'office'. God's faithful prophets, like Isaiah, Jeremiah, Ezekiel and others, all condemn the priests for their corruption and failure to teach the people God's law. Likewise, they condemn false prophets who constantly reassured the people that all was well (cf. v. 14).

And so the city that had forsaken God was now itself utterly Godforsaken. The word of God, which they had heard for centuries and had so persistently rejected, falls silent: *the law is no more, and her prophets no longer find visions from the* Lord, and *the elders,* with no wisdom to offer, can do nothing more than *sit on the ground in silence,* reduced to the same rubble as the wretched *young women* (10). Jeremiah had foreseen a future in which old men and young women would once again rejoice under

God's blessing (Jer. 31:13), but for these ones – old and young alike – caught up in the catastrophic crumbling of their whole world, that was a future they would not see. In *silence* and *sackcloth* they sink down to the streets of their sunken city, down to the dust of the earth.

2. Children dying in the streets (2:11–19)

Whether or not there is growing *anger* in the Poet's account of what has happened to Jerusalem, there is an overwhelming *grief* welling up within him and it now bursts out in an uncontrollable gush of words. The sudden shift to the first person implies that he can contain himself no longer behind the cool objectivity of third-person observation. If the plight of the old men and young girls has moved him (10), there is worse to come – infant children literally starving to death *in their mothers' arms*.

a. Unbearable sights (2:11–12)

The Poet voices his pain in a rush of physical emotion. His eyes are exhausted with weeping. His stomach is churning over. He is retching with revulsion at what he sees. What is *poured out* in 11b is not actually his *heart*, but his 'bile' – which suggests that he is literally sick and vomiting with grief and shock. And the cause is not just the destruction of a whole city, but *because my people are destroyed*. And worst of all, he sees the tiniest of children fainting with hunger, not in the privacy of their own homes (which are probably destroyed), but out *in the streets of the city* (11c, repeated 12b).[19] There in gaunt public exposure, visible and vulnerable, they are crying out to their mothers for food and drink,[20] but *their lives ebb away in their mothers' arms* (12c; Heb. 'on their mothers' breasts'). The words bring tears to our eyes just reading them. Many of us have wept at the sight of such starving, sick, wounded and dying children on our TV screens. Some of us may have witnessed it first-hand in our own countries. The sight and the grief seem too much for human hearts to bear.[21] This man, this Poet, is in

---

[19] The suffering and death of children is a noticeable part of the catalogue of curses foreseen in Deut. 28:41, 50, 53–57.

[20] It is pedantic to ask why children would ask for bread and *wine*. The two go together as a stock phrase for basic food. 'In African terms, the children are asking for fish and attiéké (a dish made with grated cassava), or bread and cheese. These are foods that belong together. "Bread and wine" is the last dream of these small victims of adult politics; and with that dream, they die' (Coulibaly, pp. 951–958).

[21] Many wept with Chris Gunness, spokesperson for the United Nations Relief and Works Agency, who broke down sobbing with his head in his hands at the end of a TV interview in the aftermath of the shelling of one of the agency's schools allegedly by the Israel Defense Force in Gaza in July 2014, in which fifteen Palestinian

the deepest agony of distress. 'The verse thus reads like a silent reproach to the Almighty: "No matter how justified your dealings with Jerusalem may be, what have these little ones done to suffer so much?"'[22]

'This man' – who is he? The weeping Poet immediately reminds us of the weeping prophet.[23] In fact, the language of verse 11 (and many of the phrases in vv. 11–19) are so reminiscent of Jeremiah that some commentators would attribute this part of the poem to Jeremiah.[24] If Jeremiah were the one who composed the poems of Lamentations, this would be no problem, of course. But if not, then whoever the anonymous Poet is, he knew the cadences of Jeremiah's passionate poetry very intimately and felt the same profound emotions.

'This *man*' – only a man? Could it be that this is the one place in the book where we hear the voice of God? It is well known that the tears of Jeremiah were the tears of God. That is to say, when we encounter the first person ('I', 'me') in some of the more passionate poetry of Jeremiah, it is often difficult to decide whether it is the prophet or God speaking. The ambiguity is surely quite intentional, for prophets were people who not only said what God wanted to be said, but also felt what God was feeling. Their emotions reflected the heart of God. So, for example, when we read, 'Since my people are crushed, I am crushed; I mourn, and horror grips me', are we hearing the voice of Jeremiah or God, or both? A few verses later, the word 'me' is undoubtedly God (Jer. 8:21; 9:3). And when we read: 'I will weep and wail for the mountains and take up a lament . . .', the voice is unquestionably God's, for God is the one speaking immediately before and after, threatening punishment and saying, 'I will make Jerusalem a heap of ruins' (Jer. 9:9–11).

Well, now God has done exactly that. So if the reality of divine anger has invaded Judah's history, the outpouring of divine grief has accompanied it. This is an unforgettable part of the message of the book of Jeremiah. God's anger is saturated with God's grief and soaked in tears both human and divine. Could it be that the book of Lamentations senses this too, and discerns the tears of God behind the weeping eyes of the Poet? Certainly, the physical symptoms of tears and sickness (11) are the Poet's, but the Poet

---

children died. Later Gunness commented, 'It's important to humanize the statistics and to realize that there is a human being with a heart and soul behind each statistic and that the humanity that lies behind these statistics should never be forgotten.' That is precisely what Lamentations does for Jerusalem's children in 587 BC.

[22] Re'emi, p. 97.

[23] The most obvious comparisons are with Jer. 8:21 – 9:1; 13:17; 14:17.

[24] The significant similarities to Jeremiah are listed by Paul House, who then adds, 'This prophetic figure [i.e. the speaker in Lamentations] weeps for the people as only one who has ministered to them can' (p. 385).

is not the only one lamenting when *my people* are destroyed and when mothers clasp dying infants to their despairing breasts. We may find some support for this possibility when we come to 3:31–36.

b. Beyond compare and beyond healing (2:13)

In another brilliant twist in the dramatic nature of this poetry, the Poet turns from his own tormented grief to the one whose incomprehensibly dreadful suffering was the cause of it. For the first time, he speaks directly to Lady Zion. In fact, it is the first time anybody has spoken to her, or even seemed to listen to her. 'Look and see,' she had pleaded; 'Is any suffering like my suffering?' (1:12). She had heard no answer yet, human or divine. But now, at last, the Poet himself comes alongside her, for he at least certainly *has* seen. He has seen so much that he is sick to the stomach. The Poet becomes the answer to the appeal within his own poem, and compels us the readers to join him in silent witness.

'Witness', indeed, is the meaning of the Poet's opening question: *What can I say for you?* – not just 'to you'. The Poet wants to speak up on her behalf, to be her advocate, to bear witness to all she is suffering. But what can he say? – it seems beyond all reasonable testimony. All through chapter 1 we heard the refrain 'There is no one to comfort her.' Now at last the Poet himself will try. But how can he do so?

One form of comfort to a suffering person (even though it is usually a rather thin and unhelpful line of approach) is to share similar sufferings of one's own or others, to offer some comparable tale of woe that reassures the sufferer that he or she is neither unique nor alone in the pain. But the Poet can offer nothing of the sort. *With what can I compare you . . . ? To what can I liken you, that I may comfort you . . . ?* There is no answer. Jerusalem's suffering is beyond comparison and beyond comfort. Or rather, the only comparison he can think of merely magnifies the enormity of it all. *Your wound is as deep as the sea.* The sea – symbol of all that is unbounded, infinite, chaotic and beyond measurement.[25] Any wound as deep as the ocean is surely beyond healing.[26]

---

[25] Immeasurable, that is, except by God. One way of expressing the infinity of God was to portray him as the one who *has* measured the oceans, and holds them, as it were, in a jam jar (Isa. 40:12; Ps. 33:7).

[26] 'The poet searches for a way to serve as a witness, to verify the extent of the destruction, to reify it, to capture it in words – and through his verbal expression to bring comfort to Jerusalem. But the catastrophe is so enormous that there is neither a historical precedent nor a phenomenon in nature against which to measure it. Nothing like it has ever happened. Its scope is unimaginable. The only image that the poet can conjure up to convey it is the vastness of the sea, which is to say that it is infinite' (Berlin, p. 73).

The language of wounds and healing (13c) is strongly reminiscent of Jeremiah (e.g. Jer. 6:14; 8:11, 22; 10:19; 14:17; 15:18). A passage in that book that comes very close to the thoughts of Lamentations 2 is Jeremiah 30:12–17. It is a beautiful text that begins with exactly what we read here:

> Your wound is incurable,
>> your injury beyond healing.
> There is no one to plead your cause,
>> no remedy for your sore,
>> no healing for you.
> All your allies [lovers] have forgotten you;
>> they care nothing for you.
> I have struck you as an enemy would . . .
> (Jer. 30:12–14)

Jeremiah then went on to promise complete reversal, accomplished by God's sovereign grace alone – a reversal that would spell God's judgment on those enemies and God's healing for his stricken people.

> 'I will restore you to health
>> and heal your wounds,'
>>> declares the LORD.
> (Jer. 30:17)

But the horizon of the Poet and Lady Zion in the tear-stained dialogue of Lamentations 2:13 has not yet stretched that far. All they can see is a devastating wound that is beyond any possibility of healing. What else could they envisage amidst the smoking ruins of their city and a countryside torn up and trampled down?

> *Your wound is as deep as the sea.*
>> *Who can heal you?*

c. False friends, fierce enemies (2:14–16)

That last rhetorical question, *Who can heal you?*, invites the various potential answers that follow – each of which proves negative. Israel had *prophets* (14); could they not have healed her? Israel had neighbours (15); could they not have helped? Israel had *enemies*, for sure (16); but might they not have exercised some mercy in their triumph? No, no and triple no.

The failure of the false prophets to warn Israel of God's threatened judgment, and thereby to *ward off* their *captivity*, is not offered as an excuse, even if it is some mitigation (14). We know all about the many other prophets in Israel in the century or more before the final destruction of Judah who betrayed and prostituted their calling (to the extent that they had one at all). Instead of warning Israel (as the true prophets of God consistently did), *they did not expose your sin*, or call for repentance. On the contrary, they assured Israel that all was well. In Jeremiah's famous and repeated words,

> Prophets and priests alike,
>   all practise deceit.
> They dress the wound of my people
>   as though it were not serious.
> 'Peace, peace,' they say,
>   when there is no peace.[27]

However, even if the words of those prophets had been *false and worthless . . . and misleading*, the people could not claim that they had been blindly duped with no other option offered to them. For God had spoken to them for forty years through Jeremiah, but they had deliberately chosen to reject his word, not to recognize and repent of the sin that he so thoroughly exposed. They were, in Paul's words, 'without excuse'.

So those prophets could not heal Lady Zion (14). But there was a prophet, Jeremiah, who had already spoken of God's healing. Could his word prevail?

We have met the 'passers-by' (15) already, in 1:12, when Lady Zion called out for them to look and sympathize with her suffering. The phrase may be generic – meaning anybody who happens to hear about what has befallen Jerusalem. But it may refer more specifically to people from neighbouring nations, those who lived closest to her, and would indeed 'pass by' and see the devastation of a once beautiful city.

Back in 1:12, they said nothing in response to her plea, but now they do. The gestures (clapping the hands and shaking the head), and the rhetorical

---

[27] Jer. 6:13–14; cf. 8:11; 14:13–16; 23:9–40; Ezek. 13:1–16. 'Unfortunately the same situation arises in many African countries ravaged by civil wars and natural calamities. Numerous "prophets" arise and hold forth day and night. But when we listen to them carefully, we recognize on the one hand that their "prophecies" are often contradictory (which is proof that some of them lie), and on the other hand, many of the prophets are simply seeking fame so that they can eat! This dramatic situation highlights the church's failure to be the lighthouse that the entire nation seeks' (Coulibaly, pp. 951–958).

question they ask, may imply mockery (*they scoff*), but they could express simple shocked amazement. Jerusalem had a reputation as a particularly beautiful city in its elevated location, and that reputation may well have been more than merely its own national boast. At any rate, whether in sarcasm or shock, the passers-by quote Psalm 48:2, and turn it upside down (15c). It would be worth pausing to read the whole of Psalm 48, and imagine how its grand claims would have felt right now, in the midst of what Lamentations 2 describes. 'How are the mighty fallen', indeed.

So their neighbours could not heal Lady Zion (15). But could the God who, according to that same psalm, 'has shown himself to be her fortress' be her healing when all her physical fortresses were reduced to rubble?

We have met the *enemies* before as well (16). We cringed from their raping, burning, trapping, tying and trampling (1:7–10, 13–15). We heard Lady Zion cry out for God to judge them too (1:22). We expect little mercy or healing from that quarter, and indeed we find none. They are not only claiming victory, they are gloating in it as something they had wanted for a long time and have now at last achieved – to their great satisfaction (16). We were told in 2:2 that God had *swallowed up* the whole country. Now we meet (though we knew already) the human *mouths* and throats that did the swallowing, and claimed credit for it themselves – Babylon's boast: *We have swallowed her up.*

So their enemies, mocking and merciless, will not heal Lady Zion (16). But could the One who had struck them as their Enemy turn his face towards them again in mercy?

This triple and ruthless removal of all possible sources of *human* help drives the logic onwards towards the only other refuge. 'Who can heal you?' (13c) – only God himself.

When other helpers fail and comforts flee,
Help of the helpless, O abide with me.[28]

But since God is the one who has inflicted the wound, can God be the one to heal it? To which the Poet's answer is a desperate final urging: 'Try it and see. There is nowhere else to go' (19).[29]

---

[28] From the hymn 'Abide with Me', by Henry Francis Lyte, 1847.

[29] 'The narrator asked in 2:13, "Who can heal you?" In 2:14 we saw that the prophets did not, in 2:15 that the passers-by could not, in 2:16 that the enemy would not, and now, in 2:17 that yhwh is himself the very one who inflicted the wound' (Parry, p. 83).

d. God has done it; cry to him! (2:17–19)

At first, the Poet's own response to the dire helplessness that he has outlined to Lady Zion appears to hold no comfort (if that is what he was trying to bring). *The LORD has done what he planned; he has fulfilled his word, which he decreed long ago* (17). As we saw in the introduction to the chapter, this is not accusing God of 'malice aforethought' – some viciously secret plan that has only now been exposed in all its horror. All he means is that the abundant warnings that Israel had received from the full canon of Torah and Prophets have now worked themselves out in terrifying historical reality. The victory of their enemies has simply been the victory of God's prevailing word – a word that has indeed prevailed over all the obfuscating words of false prophets.[30] This perspective on the calamity of 587 BC and the exile is exactly what we later read in Zechariah 1:1–6, where the same language of what God 'determined to do' is found. 'Zion's enemies are but the players on the stage. It is God who directs the action.'[31]

But theological reflection, valid and vital though it had to be, quickly gives way to the resurging emotional pain of what the Poet is witnessing. He hears people crying out to the Lord (18), and he urges Lady Zion to join them – urgently and relentlessly. He personifies the very wall of the city – now broken down in rubble – and summons it to weep day and night before God. Seven imperatives give urgent pace and persuasion to the Poet's plea, four of them coming one after the other in verse 19: *Arise, cry out . . . pour out your heart . . . lift up your hands . . .* This is the most impassioned plea in the book, addressed by the Poet to Lady Zion herself: telling her, urging her, pleading with her, to turn to the One who had inflicted such pain upon her. And if she will not plead for herself, let her plead for the sake of her children. The Poet returns to the scene that had so sickened him at the start of his speech – children dying in the street in their mothers' arms (11–12).[32] He cannot get that picture out of his mind, and now he holds it up, as it were, to Lady Zion's own weeping eyes, and says: 'Plead with God *for the lives of your children*', your dying children (19c).

One imagines that the Poet's insistence that Lady Zion should pray to the Lord is so pressing because the thing seemed so impossible – indeed

---

[30] See, for example, among many similar statements, Jer. 4:27–28.

[31] Provan, p. 75.

[32] 'In the iron age of war, an iron law is promulgated; it is the children who die first. War is mass cannibalism; we eat our own future. In the horrid banquet, all, victor and vanquished, have sordid part' (Berrigan, p. 61).

almost monstrously inappropriate. Why should the victim plead with the abuser himself for justice? Israel's monotheism here wrestles in its own dilemma. Israel cannot plead for justice from some other god against the God whose hands have struck her so violently. 'Acknowledge and take to heart this day that the LORD is God in heaven above and on the earth below. There is no other' (Deut. 4:39). No other! No other God than YHWH had judged and demolished her. No other God than YHWH could save and heal her. No other God, in heaven or on earth, to whom she must turn in the midst of the dust and death and darkness of 'the day of the LORD's anger'. But turn to him! 'Pray anyway!'[33]

3. A cry from the heart of darkness (2:20–22)

I sense a long, dramatic silence between the end of verse 19 and the beginning of verse 20. The Poet's speech has ended with a crescendo of appeal, straining every nerve and emotion, every picture of the imagination, to get Lady Zion to open her mouth and cry out to God. And after an agonized suspense, at last she does – though I imagine it not as a cry, but once again as a desperately quiet and broken voice, straining to get her tortured words out through her tears.

But if we were expecting words of repentance and then, on the basis of that, a request for mercy, pardon and restoration – we are disappointed. Lady Zion has affirmed what she knows in her head to be the truth (1:18a), but her emotions have not yet caught up with her theology. She cannot yet ask God to heal or forgive or save; all she wants is for God to *look . . . and consider* (20a). That, of course, is what she has asked for three times already (1:9c, 11c, 20a), but has had no reply. It seems she cannot yet turn to God as a friend to comfort and heal when she is still suffering the handiwork of God as her enemy. But does God *know* what that feels like? Is God aware of the horrors happening in her midst – horrors he has caused? Is God ever going to look and see?

So the Poet urges her to *pray* ('pour out your heart . . . lift up your hands' [19]), but all she can do is *question* – and what questions!

Rhetorical questions are just that. They are rhetorical. They aim to make a very strong, persuasive point. They are powerful 'weapons' in the right hands, for they compel the one receiving the questions to agree or

---

[33] O'Connor, pp. 126–127.

disagree, to argue back, or at least to respond in some way. They force attention. And attention is all this woman wants – from God. Why does he not see? Or if he does see, why does he not answer? How can he bear what cannot be borne? How can he allow what should not be allowed? (Notice that I am turning to rhetorical questions myself to explain Lady Zion's.)

> That women crazed by hunger should eat their own children, that prophets and priests should be slain in the sanctuary's safety . . . Is this your work, O God? Do you see what is happening here? Is this what you could have wanted?[34]

Three sharp questions in quick succession in verse 20 challenge God to 'explain himself', in the light of his own assumed moral order. Each question presses God to the very edges of extremity, and asks whether God has not in fact transgressed the most fundamental boundaries that God himself had created.

Her first question (20a) asks if God has not transgressed the boundaries of his covenant relationship with Israel. The literal words are simply: 'Whom have you treated thus?' Now there could be two ways of interpreting this. The NIV chooses one by inserting the word 'ever' – *Whom have you ever treated like this?* That puts the emphasis on the 'treatment' and rhetorically invites comparison. It suggests that what God has done to Israel is worse or greater than anything he has ever done to any other people. But were they not supposed to be his covenant people? How then could God have treated them worse than any other? It is a question, but (if we take it this way) it is a brutal allegation: 'God, you have treated us in a way that you would never treat anyone else. That is simply unfair. It does not seem that "the Judge of all the earth" is doing justice.'

The other way of interpreting the question is to put the emphasis on the word *whom*. That gives the sense: '*Who do you think* you are treating in this way? Don't you know who we are? How could you treat *us, us of all people,* like this?' In this reading, the emphasis is not so much on the 'treatment' as on the covenant relationship that is being ignored and trampled on (in their view). Lady Zion is appealing to God to 'look and consider' who it is that he has smashed to pulp as described in verses 1–10. Even if Israel

---

34 Slavitt, *Lamentations*, p. 71.

is guilty of rebellion against her covenant Lord (as she admits), has God himself not abandoned all restraint or obligation by punishing her so harshly beyond all imagining?

Her second question (20b) asks if God has not transgressed the boundaries of humanity itself. Human life, which God created, is sacred. Human parenting is the closest humans come, in their procreation, to the creational power of God himself. Children are a supreme blessing of God, a gift and a joy. So when mothers *eat their offspring, the children they have cared for*[35] – where is God when *that* happens?

Now of course, that was a ghastly horror of siege warfare, and a well-attested reality in times of acute starvation. And yes, Israel had been warned that such extreme contravention of all natural instincts would happen in their midst when the judgment of the covenant curses worked itself out through the attacks of their enemies (Deut. 28:53–57). But curses on paper or in the imagination are one thing. Actual children really being carved up as meat by despairing women is something else altogether. Lady Zion has witnessed that in her own streets. If God rules the world, should such things happen? she demands. The obvious answer to her question is, 'No, of course such things should not happen! It revolts the most basic essence of our humanity to think of it, let alone do it.' But if that is the case, how can God have brought about such an extremity of suffering that it *has* happened? Her question challenges God's government at a very profound level.

Her third question (20c) asks if God has not transgressed the boundaries of holiness. The Hebrew word order is this: 'Should [there] be killed in the sanctuary of the Lord priest and prophet?' The emphasis is on where the killing took place (in the holy place of the holy God – the place that should have been protected by his presence), and on who was killed (*priest and prophet*). The use of the generic singular without an article (not plural, 'the priests and the prophets') stresses their unique office. These were the agents through whom God was presumed to speak, and through whom God maintained the holiness of his presence in the midst of his people. The very people whom God should most have protected were slaughtered in the very place where they should have been most secure. And indeed, as verse 6 put it, God himself was the killer, even if the swords were Babylonian.

---

[35] It is not clear whether this means that mothers were reduced to cooking the carcasses of dead children, such as died in vv. 12 and 19, or actually killed and ate children (as recorded in the siege of Samaria, 2 Kgs 6:24–29).

Now we may quickly say that these were *corrupt* priests and *false* prophets, whose fate had been predicted by Jeremiah; and probably we'd be right. We can see the outworking of God's judgment in the light of his scriptural warnings. Perhaps that thought will occur to Lady Zion too, when she returns to the acknowledgment of her own sin. But for now, and in the agony of the slaughter, she confronts God with what seemed like a contradiction – the unholy slaughter of men presumed to be holy (as priests at least certainly were), by unholy pagans in a place supposed to be protected by God's own holiness. Should such things happen? Surely not. So where then is God? God the aggressor *seems*, in the depth of her darkness, to be also God the transgressor. God has done what should not be done. God has allowed what should not be allowed. God, won't you *look . . . and consider?*

No answer is spoken, by God or the Poet. So the questions are left hanging in the air, uncomfortable, stretching, contentious allegations – for her, for God, and for us.

And so Lady Zion sinks back from her salvo of questions to sheer lament (21–22). All she can see is death *in the dust of the streets*. And the one at whom she has hurled her questions is the one she knows has done it – *You have slain them . . . you have slaughtered* (21c). And whom had God slain? Here comes her parting shot in this prayer that isn't really a prayer at all, for she has not actually asked for anything (as urged to do by the Poet), but merely thrown her situation, her suffering and her questions at the Lord's feet and asked that he take a look (perhaps that is prayer too, of course).

They were *my young men and young women*, she cries (21b), and *you have slain them*. They were *those I cared for and reared* (22c). This is a harsh and painful distancing between Jerusalem and God, in the poetic personification of the city. For we know full well from frequent exclamations in Jeremiah just how much God loved his own people, how lovingly God had led them like a young bride on her honeymoon (Jer. 2:2), how tenderly God yearned for them, how broken-hearted God was by the suffering that was about to be inflicted on them – his own poor people. 'Oh *my* people, *my* people,' God had wept (Jer. 8:18 – 9:3).

But here, Jerusalem claims the people as though they were hers alone. Lady Zion, like Rachel, weeps for her children, for they are no more. And, worst of all, if YHWH has come against this people ('my people' in the mind and mouth of Jerusalem) – then God has become the enemy. Not just 'the' enemy, but *my enemy*.

That last line of the chapter is poignant with irony, pathos and pain: *Those I cared for and reared my enemy has destroyed* (22c). For of course, that enemy was Babylon. But behind Babylon, Lady Zion sees an enemy worse than any human empire – the Lord God himself. That is who she means by that chilling word *my enemy*. That is what she calls her God. Is that then her final riposte to the Poet who has urged her to pray to the Lord? It is an agonized and unresolved ending to the chapter. How can I pray to *my enemy* who has done this to *my* people?

But in the end – what else can she do? Where else can she turn? We shall find out in chapter 5.

Reflections

1. 'The historical lesson, stated succinctly, is that nothing made by human hands can save – not even something as significant as the house of the Lord.'[36] What are the things that Christians, as individuals or as a whole church, might be tempted to trust in and consider indestructible – with a false sense of security that God may have to destroy?

2. 'This poem raises the important matters of divine severity, human responsibility, and innocent suffering because of the actions of the wicked . . . This chapter and this book as a whole relate a message hard to bear, read, or accept: when the day of the Lord comes, one can only cry out to God in a way that confesses sin, asks questions about suffering, and intercedes on behalf of the innocent.'[37] How do you balance the three responses at the end of Paul House's comment? Should these be part of the church's response to evil in the world and the reality of God's anticipated judgment?

---

[36] Dearman, p. 453.
[37] House, p. 398.

Lamentations 3:1–66

3. Hope in the pit of despair

Lady Zion falls silent. She does not speak again in the rest of the book. She has done as the Poet urged her and addressed her cry to the Lord (2:20–22) – though hardly with the tone and specific requests he hoped for (2:18–19). Now the Poet, almost in frustration at Lady Zion's agonized brevity, bursts out of his shell of anonymity and announces himself (3:1) and the torments he has endured (1–18). Well, not quite leaving anonymity behind, since he does not give us his name, but he certainly tells us who is speaking and why – assuming, as I do, that the speaker in this chapter is the same as the Poet who has been guiding our thoughts so far. *'This is me, now,'* he seems to say.

The identity of this voice that suddenly and passionately declares *I am the man who has seen affliction* (1) is much debated. For those who see Lamentations as a collection of unrelated poems of lament, he is regarded as an anonymous voice, completely different from any of the rest in the book. For those who see an intentional coherence and unity amidst the swirling, pain-soaked poetry of the book, it seems much more likely that this voice is intended to be heard as coming from the same person who narrates chapters 1 and 2. The key difference is that, whereas in those chapters he has described the suffering of the city of Jerusalem objectively either in the third person or sometimes in the second person, when addressing Lady Zion herself, here he makes it first person singular ('This is me'). He is not just an observer of the city's suffering; he himself has participated in it to the fullest degree. He was there. And so the whole first part of the chapter (1–24), and the final section (52–66), are personal testimony.

So who is he? Answer: we don't know, but not for want of guessing. Traditionally, he was identified as Jeremiah, by those who regard the whole book as coming from the weeping prophet. And even those who think it highly unlikely that Jeremiah is the author of Lamentations cannot but agree that this chapter is full of language, images, emotions and even experience that are unquestionably Jeremiah-like. So some think that the author of this chapter (whoever he was) is deliberately assuming the guise or persona of an idealized Jeremiah. Other identifications with historical figures in the Old Testament (such as Zedekiah or Baruch) are pure speculation. Rather than trying to name him, many contemporary commentators regard *the man* as a representative figure, on the one hand embodying the suffering of the city and its people (for he has participated in it), and yet, on the other hand, offering to them (as is the custom of some prophets and lament psalms) a fresh perspective, some theological wrestling, a call to repentance and foundations for renewed hope.[1]

However, he is not *merely* representative of the city and people. Certainly, he speaks *for* them and describes their suffering as his own (in vv. 1–18 especially). That is his integrity and authenticity; he speaks from the inside. Yet he also speaks *to* them and appeals to them and calls out to God on their behalf. In this double role – both sharing the identity of Israel (speaking *as* Israel) yet also speaking and acting *towards* Israel and on their behalf – this figure has something in common with the Servant of the Lord in Isaiah also.[2] And indeed, that kind of double role was laid on some of the prophets. They were called, in some cases, to embody in their own life experience something of the reality of Israel, as well as to speak the word of God to Israel. Hosea, for example, suffers through a betrayed, broken and redeemed marriage an embodiment of Israel's journey with YHWH their covenant 'husband'. Ezekiel starved, shaved and defiled himself in a year-long portrayal of the suffering of Judah under the wrath of God. Jeremiah felt in the depths of his being not only the anger and anguish of God, but also the terrible suffering of Israel that he foresaw and forewarned about for forty years.

---

[1] For a full discussion of the various scholarly suggestions for the identity of the speaker in ch. 3, see House, pp. 405–408; Parry, pp. 91–96.

[2] 'We have met this figure of loss before. The one lamenting is the "I" of Job, or the suffering servant of Second Isaiah, or Jeremiah in the pit. He is Jesus in the days of His passion' (Berrigan, p. 66). See also the Introduction, section 4, pp. 29–33.

All that being so, it would not be difficult, in my view, to regard the author of this chapter (and the book) as speaking *both* as a personified representative figure (speaking, that is, as suffering Israel), *and* also in his own capacity as the prophetic poet who sought to give full utterance to unimaginable suffering and yet at the same time to shed the light of hope into the darkness of the pit. Nor would it be difficult (again, in my own view, as in the Introduction) to imagine Jeremiah himself doing both of those things in the powerful poetry of this chapter (since he did them both often enough in the book that bears his name). However, presumably for good reason, *the man* does *not* tell us his name, and so we should honour his anonymity. Let's simply call him what he calls himself – 'the Man'.[3]

'Powerful poetry' – it certainly is. This central chapter of the book parades its own centrality by heightening and sharpening the acrostic device. In chapters 1 and 2, the three-line stanzas (in Hebrew), represented by a single verse (in English), begin with successive letters of the Hebrew alphabet at the start of the first line only. In chapter 3, however, the Poet produces stanzas where all three lines begin with the same letter of the alphabet. Since the addition of verse numbers to the Hebrew text, each of the single lines is given a single verse – with the result that in our Bibles Lamentations 3 has sixty-six one-line verses, even though it is the same length as each of chapters 1 and 2, with their twenty-two three-line verses.[4] The constant repetition of opening consonants, and occasionally of whole words (25–27, 'good . . . good . . . good'; 31–33, 'for . . . for . . . for'), produces a punchy, staccato effect that is enhanced by the fact that the lines themselves are often shorter than in chapters 1 and 2.

However, the flow of meaning is not parcelled up or boxed in by these three-line stanzas. The Man sometimes produces a sudden change of direction in the third line of a stanza (as in 21, 42), or carries a metaphor across from the end of one stanza to the start of another (known as 'enjambment'; as at 12–13, 15–16, 45–46, 48–49, 60–61). And the chapter

---

[3] The word is emphatic in position and meaning. It is not either of the common words for a male human, *'ādām* or *'îš*. It is *geber*, which is used of men in their strength and vigour, particularly soldiers. Some translate it as 'the strongman' (O'Connor), or 'the Valiant Man' (Parry). There is much speculation as to why the author chooses this word (in v. 1 and again in v. 39). Perhaps it is a deliberate 'contradiction in terms'. If he is a strong man, one who should have defended and protected his loved ones, why has he ended up in utter weakness, humiliated, bound and tortured (1–18)?

[4] And since ch. 4 has twenty-two two-line verses, and ch. 5 has twenty-two one-line verses, the result is that ch. 3 is the same length as chapters 4 and 5 combined.

as a whole is a 'sandwich' in which the outer layers are wrapped in wrath (1, 66) and extreme suffering, while the centre holds words of affirmation and hope (22–24, 31–33).

That 'sandwich' effect is emotionally and theologically significant. For it is only in this chapter that we hear any words of hope at all.[5] And they are words from the ocean depths of Israel's faith and Israel's God. But they are surrounded on both sides by words of uncomforted pain, not-yet-forgiven sin, and continuing suffering. So, as we read and reread this chapter, we oscillate with the Poet himself between two vast realities – human suffering and evil, and divine compassion and goodness. We cannot struggle through the horrors of verses 1–18 without knowing that verses 22–24 and 31–33 are coming up soon. But equally, we cannot soak in the warmth of those verses without knowing that very soon our eyes will be streaming with tears at the destruction of the people (48). The same voice that appeals to God's steadfast love for those who wait for him (22–26) also appeals to God's retributive justice for his enemies (64–66). But equally, the same voice that claims to have lost all hope from the Lord (18) also reports that in his extremity God had spoken two words to him – the only words of God in the whole book – 'Do not fear' (57).

This counterbalancing of two vast realities is important, for we should not allow either to diminish, still less dismiss, the other. On the one extreme, one might focus so predominantly on the words of hope and assurance in the centre of Lamentations 3, or assert that they are the 'real message' of the book, that one undermines the integrity of the voices of suffering that surround them – especially when we add chapters 1–2 and 4–5 to the 'sandwich'. There is certainly nourishing faith and hope at the heart of the book, but we arrive at it and depart from it along roads of intense pain. And the Poet is still walking that road even as the book ends. So we trivialize that pain if we set it all to one side and dig out only the hope at the centre. If we do that, we merely collude with those who pass by and leave Zion comfortless (ch. 1). And that is indeed what has happened to the book of Lamentations itself – unread, unvisited by many (if not most) Christians, certainly in the comfortable West. The only part of the book many people even know at all is 3:22–24 – and that, not because they have read Lamentations or know the surrounding context, but only from songs such as 'The Steadfast Love of the Lord Never Ceases'

---

[5] With the single exception of 4:22.

by Edith McNeill or that old favourite hymn by Thomas Chisholm, 'Great Is Thy Faithfulness'.

At the other extreme lies the danger of so over-reacting *against* such superficial claiming of 3:22–24 as a fast-acting analgesic to all the surrounding pain, that one leaves the pain and suffering unsoftened, uncomforted by the hope of any resolution – ever. On this view, it is the suffering voice that simply overwhelms the glimmers of hope in the middle of chapter 3. The affirmation of God's faithfulness is neutralized by the questioning, protesting voice that accuses God of the opposite. If the heart of the book is an attempt at theodicy, it fails. The challenge to God's character that is hurled at him by the suffering of the world simply overwhelms the attempted defence of God's goodness and governance.

That is the view of Kathleen O'Connor (though she holds it somewhat tentatively and in the context of personal suffering mixed with faith and hope). First of all, she disputes the idea that verses 3:22–33 are central to the book as a whole, and therefore its intended primary message. For although they come in the middle of chapter 3, chapters 4 and 5 not only reassert the pain and suffering, but they are also progressively shorter[6] and the acrostic form is abandoned in chapter 5. The book limps to its questioning finish. She goes on,

> These asymmetries disturb the seeming dominance of the strongman's voice and dump cold water on optimists seeking a quick escape from the book's painful world. Hope appears as an important interlude, a moment of calm in the storm, but merely one perspective among several in the aftermath of the invasion.
>
> . . . The strongman's hopeful testimony is fragile and uncertain. He vacillates so often between hope and despair that his hope remains ambiguous at best. This is not to deny the presence of hope in the poem but rather to question a long history of interpretation where hope washes away and silences the suffering and despair around it. It is not clear that hope is the book's radiant center nor that a theology of explicit hope dominates the book.
>
> Instead, the realities of suffering and death and of a God remembered rather than encountered repeatedly moderate and overcome hope.[7]

---

[6] Ch. 4 has two-line verses, and ch. 5 one-line verses.

[7] O'Connor, p. 45.

There is a lot of truth in that perception. But I come back to the need to affirm *both* great realities, doing full justice to the integrity of both – the horror of suffering and evil which must be fully expressed and remembered, *and* the abiding faithfulness and goodness of God which anchors the soul. To recognize and affirm each one is not to limit or 'wash away' the other. Each exists in its entirety and each challenges the other. The fact that when the continent meets the ocean, at that point it is reduced to sand on the shore by the power of the ocean does not deny the reality of the continent as a whole. Neither does the fact that the ocean is reduced to tiny ripples by the beach deny the reality of the ocean's vast depths and billows.

In the end, however, which will overcome the other and be the eternal reality – evil, suffering, pain and death? Or the faithfulness, mercy and goodness of God? We need more than this book alone to answer that question, though it does point us through the dark mists of its own suffering to the light of hope. For that reason, I am taking that word 'hope' from where it occurs several times in the centre of the chapter, and letting it speak for itself through the voice of the Man.

1. Hope perishing: The Man voices his people's experience (3:1–18)

The first part of chapter 3 is similar to the first part of chapter 2 – describing the destruction of Jerusalem. In both chapters the subject of the barrage of verbs and metaphors is 'he' – that is, God (although he is not named in ch. 3 until v. 18). But the difference is that whereas chapter 2 describes the destruction objectively in the third person, in chapter 3 the Man speaks in the first person, which greatly intensifies the sense of traumatic violent assault by God himself. 'This is what God has done *to me!*'

I am the man who has seen affliction by the rod of the Lord's wrath (1). The Man speaks out of experience that is both personal and corporate. What he describes through a series of increasingly terrifying metaphors is, of course, the suffering of the siege of Jerusalem, the final collapse and destruction of the whole city, the death of many, and then the hopeless fate of exile. But by speaking in the first person singular (*I, me*), he not only personifies the city, but makes its suffering his own – which it had been. It is as though, having failed to get Lady Zion to say anything more herself by the end of chapter 2, he now speaks up for her, identifying with her suffering as something he too has shared. What we have here, in my view, is the merging of the voice of a 'character' in the dramatic poetry of the book (the conversation partner with Lady Zion in chs. 1–2) with the voice of the author of the book itself.

The Man is the Poet.

a. The Lord as a rogue shepherd (3:1–6)[8]

The rod (*šēbeṭ*) was a shepherd's club (1). It is a word used in various ways (including the sceptre of authority and a rod of punishment[9]). But its most famous use is in Psalm 23, where David portrays the Lord as the shepherd whose 'rod and . . . staff' are comforting, because when the sheep sees them it knows that the shepherd has the equipment to protect it from any attacking animal (Ps. 23:4). For that reason, the sheep has no fear of evil.

The shepherd's 'rod'/club would have been a stout piece of wood, perhaps just over a metre in length (like a baseball bat), often with a heavy end that might have been strengthened with pieces of metal or stone. It was a weapon, not a walking stick (that was the 'staff'), and in the hands of a strong man,[10] it was a very effective one against most wild animals that might attempt to savage a sheep.

The sharp irony of these verses, therefore, is that the shepherd's club has mutated from a comforting symbol of protection into a bruising weapon of attack. God the good shepherd, using his club to defend his sheep, has morphed into a rogue shepherd whacking his own flock with his club.

The inverted shepherding metaphor persists through these verses in various ways. A good shepherd would gather his sheep together and lead them through dark places to the sunshine. This 'shepherd' has done the opposite of both (2). Hands that should tend and care for the sheep have been *turned . . . against* them repeatedly (3). Rather than protect the sheep and bind their wounds and injuries, this 'shepherd' has inflicted devastating injuries on them himself (4).[11] The good shepherd leads his

---

[8] The 'bad shepherd' motif in these verses was observed by Hillers, p. 124, and adopted by Berlin, p. 86.

[9] Isaiah uses the word to describe Assyria (Isa. 10:5) as a rod/club in the hands of YHWH, through whom he was punishing Judah. The painful truth now is that God is doing the same thing again to Jerusalem, though even more catastrophically and terminally, through Babylon.

[10] Or even a determined youth; it may well have been such a club that David used to strike the lion and bear he claims to have killed to rescue his father's sheep (1 Sam. 17:34–37).

[11] This is a sharp inversion of Ezek. 34. God has behaved towards his people like the 'bad shepherds' he accused of mistreating them (Ezek. 34:4).

sheep out of danger, and guides them through the dark valley of the shadow of death. This 'shepherd' surrounds them with *bitterness and hardship* (5), and leaves them stranded in the place of darkness and death (6).[12]

b. Walled up alive (3:7–9)

God morphs yet again, from rogue shepherd to cruel jailer. The Man describes the claustrophobic feeling of imprisonment without hope of escape or appeal. He is *walled . . . in*, chained down and blocked off. The walls are so thick that even his cries for help cannot be heard – deliberately (8). The prison is built with 'cut stone' (9) – that is to say: these walls are not just hastily erected dry-stone walls that could be pushed down with effort. They are deliberately constructed by the divine engineer out of closely fitting hewn stones that are impenetrable. Israelites trapped in Jerusalem had no way of escape from the besieging Babylonians, no hope of help from human allies, and no prayer that could reach their ultimate Enemy.

We don't know if Jeremiah was chained while he was imprisoned in the military quarters of the palace during the siege, but the language here certainly reflects the experience of being imprisoned by his own people within a city that was itself imprisoned by an implacable enemy within a siege (Jer. 32:1–2; 33:1).

c. Hunted to death (3:10–13)

The images shift rapidly. Perhaps we are back in the shepherd motif again. Rather than God being the shepherd who, like young David, would protect his sheep from *a bear* or *a lion*, he has become one of those wild beasts, *lying in wait*, and then pouncing on the sheep, dragging it *from the path* and tearing it to pieces. And since the protecting shepherd has defected to join the attacking claws and jaws, the sheep is indeed *without help* (10–11). There is a nightmare quality to the sequence of thought. 'If the speaker ever did get out of prison a terrible beast would attack him (see Amos 5:18–20).'[13]

But perhaps the shepherd has a bow and arrows to defend the sheep from the wild animals? Indeed he does; *he drew his bow . . .* but instead of

---

[12] V. 6 is a quote from Ps. 143:3. Similar despair, connecting darkness and death, is found in Ps. 88:4–6, 18. The theme of darkness, along with the wild beasts in v. 10, may also echo the earlier reference to the day of YHWH's wrath, and Amos 5:18–20.

[13] House, p. 411. Bears and lions are common metaphors for enemies, or God acting in judgment; cf. Isa. 59:9–11; Hos. 13:8; Amos 5:19; Pss 17:12; 22:13; Jer. 4:7; 5:6; etc.

shooting the beasts, he *made me the target for his arrows . . .*! (12). The shock is terrifying. The arrows pierce the Man's vital organs (13),[14] leaving him bleeding to certain death. God as an enemy archer is an image already used in 2:4, and doubtless reflects the deadly accuracy of Babylonian soldiers in the final assault on the city.

d. Driven to despair (3:14–18)

Taunting mockery is part of the torture of the whole experience. Lady Zion has already complained of it bitterly. Here the Man says he had become *the laughing-stock of all my people* (14). Some scholars change *my people* to 'the peoples',[15] finding it odd that the personified city of Jerusalem would have been taunted by her own people. But if the Man speaks not only as the personified city but also as the voice of Jeremiah (or a Jeremiah-like figure), then certainly the mockery of his own people, even during the final months of the siege and afterwards, was a significant part of his suffering.

Extra humiliation is inflicted by a diet of bitterness[16] and dirt. It is not clear whether verse 16 implies a kind of torture in which a prisoner is forced to eat gravel, or simply portrays the act of trampling on the head of a defeated enemy ('biting the dust'). Either way, it is a grotesque picture, particularly being applied to what God has done to his own people and city.

Beaten, broken, imprisoned, mauled, shot, mocked, trampled . . . reeling under such a battery of injuries the Man reaches the point of total despair. Bereft of any kind of well-being (*šālôm*), he has *forgotten* what 'goodness' might ever be like (17).[17] The future has evaporated,[18] along with any hope he had from God (18). A future without hope is bleak indeed – no future at all. And we know the exiled survivors of 587 BC thought exactly that (e.g. Ezek. 37:11). This verse is undoubtedly the lowest, hope-less, point in the chapter – possibly the book. Hope is perishing in the very words that the Man says to himself (18).

---

[14] The word translated *heart* is actually 'my kidneys' (ESV); 'my vitals' (NRSV).

[15] It is a single-letter difference in Hebrew: *ʿammî* (MT) to *ʿammîm*.

[16] After eating *bitter herbs*, the Man is forced to drink *gall*, which refers to the juice of wormwood, a very bitter herb that elsewhere serves as a metaphor for acute sorrow (Amos 5:7; 6:12; Prov. 5:4 [ESV]). It had medicinal properties too, but that is hardly in view here.

[17] *Ṭôbâ* can mean *prosperity* (NIV), but here it probably means any enjoyment of life at any level; 'I have forgotten what happiness is' (NRSV; ESV).

[18] The word *neṣaḥ* can mean 'splendour, glory' (NIV). But it can also mean 'duration', 'perpetuity'. Hence 'my endurance' (ESV). So it could mean that the Man can simply take no more. But in the context, it seems to me that the sense is, 'My ability to see any future ahead of me has perished', i.e. 'I have lost all hope' – even hope in the Lord, as the second part of the verse explains.

But what is the last word the Man has spoken and the Poet written? The last word at the end of verse 18 is 'YHWH' – *the LORD*. At one level, this naming of God is the terrible finale to the list of grievous assaults of the previous eighteen verses – all this is what *the LORD* has done! But at another level, to name YHWH in the same breath as lamenting the loss of future and hope is oxymoronic – a contradiction in terms. With YHWH in the picture, the God who will be what he will be, there cannot *not* be a future. There cannot *not* be hope.

And so, having sunk to its very lowest point, if the poem is to continue at all, the only way is up. And this is indeed where the Man begins a painful climb, in which for every inch upwards he has to strain every sinew and muscle of faith to grasp hold of the truths deeply embedded in that one word – *the LORD*.

2. Hope remembering: The Man clings to his people's faith (3:19–39)

Israel lived by memory and hope. The whole narrative nature of Old Testament Scripture proclaims that truth. They looked back to what God had done in their past, and they looked forward to what God would do in fulfilment of the promises that had driven their past and guaranteed their future. Memory and hope dominate verses 19–39, but wildly oscillating between negative and positive.

a. Bad memory (3:19–20)

To start off with, as we have seen, all hope has gone (18) and the only memories are bad ones (19–20). Both verses 19 and 20 begin with the word *remember*. Some translations take the opening word of verse 19 as an imperative – a plea to God to remember his sufferings (ESV) – but this seems somewhat unlikely in the immediate context. More probably it is an infinitive construct, with the sense 'to remember[19] *my affliction and my wandering*[20] is *bitterness and gall*'.[21]

---

[19] 'The thought of my affliction and my homelessness is wormwood and gall!' (NRSV).

[20] This pair of words echoes 1:7, where they describe Jerusalem, heightening the effect of the Man speaking on behalf of the city. *Wandering* probably refers to the experience of exile.

[21] The phrase in the KJV, 'the wormwood and the gall', inspired a line in Edward Perronet's 1780 hymn, 'All Hail the Power of Jesus' Name': 'Sinners, whose love can ne'er forget / The wormwood and the gall, / Go, spread your trophies at his feet / And crown him Lord of all.'

That kind of memory arises unbidden. It is the natural emotional and psychological reaction to great trauma, especially the shattering violence of war – the well-attested phenomenon of unwanted flashbacks and nightmares. So verse 20 intensifies the negative memory, with the typical Hebrew structure 'remembering, my soul remembers' – that is, 'I vividly, frequently, painfully, wretchedly, continually remember . . .', until my soul sinks down into misery and depression. To have lived through, and witnessed, the final choking fires of Jerusalem and the blood-soaked slaughter or capture of its starved inhabitants must have been an ineradicable and soul-destroying memory.

b. Truth remembered (3:21–24)

But there is another kind of memory. It is the deliberate, determined, teeth-gritting decision to call something to mind. It is an action of the will, not a reaction of the emotions. It is a conscious and difficult choice: 'I *will* think about this.' That is the flavour of the remarkable verse 21 – which though it is the last line of a stanza of negative remembering (19–20), becomes the first line of a glorious positive affirmation and the turning point of the whole chapter.

> Nothing is heavier than one's head when one is struggling; raising
> one's eyes requires great effort. Yet such effort is exactly what
> is called for here. The man takes himself in hand. He makes a
> decision, voluntarily affirming his faith, and acts with resolution
> and determination.[22]

This, says the Man, with powerful contrasting emphasis, *this I call to mind* (21). But *call to mind* feels a little too weak. The Man says (Heb.), 'This I cause to return to my heart.' The heart in Hebrew is the seat not so much of the emotions as of the mind and will. The Man does not just happen to remember something. He *makes it come back* into his conscious thinking, so as to change his whole perspective. This is something he knows that he knows, and he knows that he needs to get it back into his thinking right now. Sometimes it takes a very emphatic act of will to remember what we already know, when everything in our present experience threatens to deny it and overwhelm us.

---

22 Coulibaly, pp. 951–958.

Something similar happens in the middle of Psalm 73. The author has been lamenting the prosperity of the wicked and the seeming futility of trying to live a godly life when all you get is daily afflictions (Ps. 73:1–14). But then, as we say in Northern Ireland, he catches himself on. He knows that he is thinking wrongly and if he were to voice his thoughts it would be a betrayal (15). So he goes to the place of worship, into the presence of God, and 'then I understood' (17). There is no apparent change in his circumstances, but a radical reversal of his perspective. So the psalm can confidently end where it falteringly began, by affirming the goodness of God (1, 28).

Something like that happens when the Man chooses to remember *this*. The *hope* that he thought had abandoned him for ever reappears: *therefore I have hope*. The contrast between the end of verse 18 and the last word of verse 21 is astonishing. What can he have remembered that lifts a man who says he has lost all he ever hoped for into a place where he can say *I have hope*? What is the *this* that emphatically opens verse 21?

The opening words of verse 22 are the dramatic answer. In fact, they seem to be the intended object of what he calls to mind in verse 21: 'This is what I call to mind . . . YHWH's acts of faithful love!'

This is what happens, you see, when you let YHWH's name into the text, even by the back door – as he did at the end of verse 18. Once utter the Lord's name and you cannot help remembering the multiple proofs of his covenant love. After all, it is how YHWH proclaimed his own identity at the start of Israel's journey with God: 'The LORD, the LORD, the compassionate and gracious God, slow to anger, abounding in love and faithfulness . . .' (Exod. 34:6).

That journey seemed to have come to an end in the darkness and death of 587 BC and exile. But if YHWH was still God, then it surely could not be the end. For the character of the Lord God must be as eternal as God himself. And that is what verse 22 affirms in a beautiful chiastic structure:[23]

This I call to mind . . .

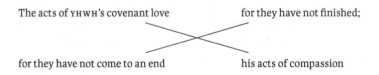

The acts of YHWH's covenant love   for they have not finished;

for they have not come to an end   his acts of compassion

---

[23] The chiastic structure of the verse is one reason for adopting the reading '*they* are not consumed', rather than the MT '*we* are not consumed' (NIV). The inverse parallelism works best with the third-person verbs repeated. See Parry, pp. 100–101.

Verse 23 turns this reality into a daily renewed reminder, *new every morning*, and comes full circle back to the greatness of God's *faithfulness*.

These verses (22–23), resonating as they do with harmonics from all over the Scriptures, are deservedly famous. It is grievous that they suffer from being so often extracted from their context in the midst of the surrounding pain of the whole book of Lamentations. But ironically, they are often quoted and sung in the midst of personal suffering and danger by believers who may know nothing of what our Poet describes – the horrors of 587 BC – but who do know personal or community suffering (illness, bereavement, poverty, persecution, war, dislocation, disaster, etc.). So, in the devotions and songs of multitudes of believers ever since, the sustaining truth at the heart of the Man's memory becomes embedded again in surrounding trauma, bringing a transforming perspective and renewed hope.

> Lamentation is not the sole response of those who believe and are
> broken.
> Or better – Lamentation also, though rarely and tentatively – smiles.
> As here. Come, urges the poet, walk with me out of the night.
> God is still God, the promise holds firm.[24]

Indeed, so psychologically and spiritually powerful is this new act of remembering that the Man forgets for a moment his self-absorption with the suffering that God ('He . . .') has afflicted him with and speaks directly to that same God – *great is* ***your*** *faithfulness*. He has not done this before. Lady Zion has addressed God, but the Poet has only ever spoken of God in the third person.[25] 'For the first time in the poem, he addresses God directly, as though God had been his silent audience all along and he knows he can turn and make contact with the divine Eavesdropper.'[26]

When he turns to more prolonged prayer in the second part of the chapter, it will be in a somewhat different tone. But when we get there we should not forget that the confession, protest and appeals that we will hear there are grounded on the solid affirmation of faith here: YHWH is the known and remembered God of proven covenant love, compassion and faithfulness – no matter what he has done, or has not yet done. *All* his

---

[24] Berrigan, p. 76.

[25] With one single exception – 1:10c. But that is more an accusation or a question than a prayer.

[26] O'Connor, p. 50.

actions must be viewed within that light, even if it strains our theology to the limits (as it will).

So the Man talks to himself yet again. In verse 18 ('So I say . . .'), he had voiced his utter loss of future and hope. Now, with his perspective transformed by what he has forced back into his mind, he can say something very different: *I say to myself, 'The LORD is my portion,'*[27] *therefore I will wait for him'* (24).[28] *I will wait* is the verb of the same root as the lost 'hope' of verse 18. 'Hope springs eternal',[29] but only when its focus is on the eternal Lord God.

c. Waiting in hope (3:25–30)

Are you ever astonished by the Bible? I hope so. For nothing seems more astonishing to me than that someone who has exploited a whole catalogue of violent metaphors to describe the suffering that God has inflicted on him (1–18) can turn round and say, *The LORD is good . . .* (25)! How on earth can he say that? Yet he does.[30] Remember, this is 'the man who has seen affliction by the rod of [his] wrath' (1). This is the man who has been stung, stifled, savaged and shot in verses 4–16. Read those scary verses again. And *nothing he says now cancels out the suffering described there*. It stands still in his memory and in our text. He does not deny it, and neither should we. But he is no longer drowning in it. For his deliberate act of remembrance has brought a moment of calm to his soul, a moment in which he reflects on some of the core truths of Israel's faith.

And the first core truth is the goodness of God – affirmed here, not in the swelling praise of Psalm 136,[31] but in the aftermath of the most horrendous suffering under the hand of God's covenant judgment. For if the

---

[27] Israelite families had their 'portion' in the land – their inheritance from generation to generation. The Levites, however, were given no territory as their allotted portion of land (so they were dependent on the tithes, firstfruits and offerings of the landed population). Instead, they were told, the Lord himself was their portion (Num. 18:20). They could live without land, so long as they had the Lord. That background may be what gives the Man hope. Even without land, city, king or temple, he had the Lord. A friend who worked in Rwanda shortly after the genocide there told me of meeting a man, destitute by the roadside, who had lost his whole family and home. His words were unforgettable: 'I never knew Jesus was all I needed till Jesus was all I had.'

[28] This is another echo of the dynamic shift of mood in Ps. 73; see Ps. 73:26.

[29] Alexander Pope.

[30] Indeed, the Poet emphasizes his point by triple repetition of the word *good* (*ṭôb*) at the start of every line of the stanza beginning with the Hebrew letter *tet* (25–27) – *good . . . good . . . good*. This stanza and the next but one (31–33; 'for . . . for . . . for') are the only two stanzas in the poem that use this device of triple repetition of whole first words, not just first letters. It gives significant weight and prominence to the content of these stanzas.

[31] And many other psalms, of course; e.g. Pss 73:1; 100:5; 106:1; 107:1; 118:1; 119:68; 135:3; 145:9.

God who punishes is the God who is good, then punishment cannot be the last word. There must be a future worth waiting for – *It is good to wait quietly for the salvation of the LORD* (26). That, of course, had been the resilient hope built into the covenant from the start. Deuteronomy 28 – 30 (and the Song of Deut. 32) had mapped out in advance the history of Israel, including the outworking of the covenant curses, whose textual horrors had now become numbing reality. *But* God was not bound by the past or boxed in by the present. The future was always open to newness of life and promise because of the unquenchable love and faithfulness of God. 'Even if you have been banished to the most distant land under the heavens, from there the LORD your God will gather you and bring you back' (Deut. 30:4). That was Deuteronomy's promise in the gloriously hope-filled chapter 30 with its evangelistic ending.

The Man cannot yet see that far ahead. He cannot even be entirely sure what future hope might look like. The best he can manage is the assertion that the right thing to do is to wait in quiet self-abasement, in the knowledge of God's goodness, and hope that the 'perhaps' of verse 29 will graduate to a clearer certainty. *There may yet be hope* (29) is not quite the negation of his earlier statements that some commentators read into it. The word 'perhaps' is clearly there in Hebrew. But it seems to me that the Poet is not so much questioning whether God ever will act in salvation (26), as simply affirming the freedom of God's sovereignty.[32] God will do what God will do; so trust him, even if you know not what or when. As Daniel's three friends said to Nebuchadnezzar: 'Our God whom we serve is able to deliver us ... *But if not* ... we will not serve your gods' (Dan. 3:17–18, ESV; my italics). There is an element of that cry of the father who brought his child to Jesus, 'I do believe; help me overcome my unbelief!' (Mark 9:24).

So the Man offers his advice to the suffering. There is something of Job, or Job's friends, in verses 27–30. At first sight, it seems ironic for this Man, who has been anything but quiet himself and who has urged Lady Zion to cry out to God, to advocate that it is *good to wait quietly ... Let him sit alone in silence* (26, 28). I think his words must not be taken with wooden literalness, as if he now regrets and denounces every syllable of protest to which he has already given vent. He is not saying that sufferers like himself should *never* speak their pain. No, there is a time for yelling out, but there

---

[32] '...A recognition that God is sovereign and cannot be treated like a blessing-dispensing machine. The prophets also sometimes spoke in terms of the *possibility* of God's salvation after judgment (Amos 5:15; Zeph. 2:3)' (Parry, p. 105).

is also a time to calm down under the recital of remembered truths. This Poet swings from one to the other without denying the validity of either. God allows (indeed encourages, by including it in Scripture) the strident voice of pain and protest – the classic outpouring of biblical lament, so common in the Psalms, so familiar to Jeremiah, and perfected here in Lamentations. But God also calls for the quiet humility of faith, born of penitence and sustained by hope. That is what emerges here in the midst of a storm that has not yet gone away and will return in force by the end of this chapter and remain unabated through the rest of the book.

d. Bedrock (3:31–33)

The astonishing contrast between the turbulent desperation of verses 1–18 and the calm depths and surprising advice of verses 22–30 demands an explanation. And here we have it. Every line of this stanza begins with *kî – For*. These verses are offered as the *reason* why the Man can speak with such calm assurance about the wisdom of humbly submitting to God even in the midst of suffering. And that reason is part of the bedrock of biblical theology.

The Poet has reached what will be the centre point of his whole book[33] and the central pillar of his theology, battered though it is by all that surrounds it. God is again the subject of the verbs, as in verses 1–18, but God's actions are modified in a way that changes the world. Three of God's actions are listed in quick succession.

- God rejects his people as an act of judgment – yes, but not *for ever* (31).
- God *brings grief* when he acts in punishment – yes, but he will again *show compassion*, because that is his abiding and abundant nature (32).
- God does indeed *bring affliction* and *grief* – yes, but it is not what his heart truly wants (33; *not willingly* is [Heb.] 'not . . . from his heart').

---

[33] I think it is valid to make this point, in spite of Kathleen O'Connor's observation that chs. 4 and 5 get progressively shorter, so that statistically (in terms of word length) this is not the middle. But since vv. 31–36 represent the middle letters of the Hebrew alphabet (*kaph* and *lamed*), in the middle of the central poem out of five, I think there is a conscious and deliberate 'centring' by the Poet here, particularly in vv. 31–33. I agree with Robin Parry: 'This stanza contains perhaps the most profound theological insight of the whole book, and its location is perhaps no coincidence. *Right at the literal center of the book of Lamentations is an appreciation of ʏʜᴡʜ as the ground of hope*' (p. 105; his italics).

Once again, the intensity and skill of the poetry are remarkable. The two outer negatives – 'not . . . for ever' (31), 'not . . . from his heart' (33) – frame the climactic central positive: 'he will have compassion according to the magnitude of his loving-kindnesses' (32). The central and eternal character of God – his compassion and faithful love – outweighs the effects of his reaction against sin and evil. So even though that reaction involves the 'recoil' effect, in which human folly and rebellion generate their own inevitable disastrous results (the judgment of God experienced through the hands of implacable destructive human enemies), that punishment will not last for ever.

There is an important theological truth here. We should not equate God's love and God's anger, as if they were both eternally equivalent attributes of deity. God's anger against evil is a terrible reality. It is the negative outworking of God's goodness in rejecting and repelling all that is contrary to his nature and will, but it is not eternally definitive of his character. God *is* love. God *is not* anger. On the contrary, God is 'slow to anger', but 'abounding in love'. The imbalance is a thousand to one, according to Deuteronomy 7:9–10. We have several verses in Scripture that tell us God's anger will not last for ever. That indeed is something that makes YHWH incomparable among all other claimed deities.

> Who is a God like you,
>> who pardons sin and forgives the transgression
>> of the remnant of his inheritance?
> *You do not stay angry for ever*
>> but delight to show mercy.
> You will again have compassion on us.[34]

Robin Parry captures the significance of these three verses very well:

> This is theology proper – an appreciation of who God is in his very being. God gets *no pleasure* from inflicting pain on people – his judgments are not the way he *wants* to relate to humanity but are his response to human sin. Punishment is an 'alien' work of God[35] given reluctantly and after

---

[34] Mic. 7:18–19; my italics. Cf. Ps. 103:9; Isa. 54:7–8. 'Not God's love, but his anger is a passing phase' (Hillers, p. 129).

[35] The concept of punishment as God's 'alien work' comes from Isa. 28:21.

numerous warnings. In his innermost self, God is full of loving kindness and mercy, and that is how he *wants* to relate to humans. Consequently, affliction is temporary and is followed by mercy. Here then is an understanding of who YHWH is, an understanding grounded in his self-revelation to Moses (Exod. 34:6–7) and his acts of mercy shown over and over again through the history of Israel (e.g. Gen. 32:11; Ps. 25:6; 89:1, 49; 106:7; 107:43; Isa. 63:7). This theology forms the basis for hope in the midst of crisis.[36]

Very true.

But the crisis remains. Theological truth and experienced suffering continue to battle each other. 'Herein lies the theological tension residing at the poem's heart. The remainder of the poem struggles with the conflict between divine rejection and divine mercy.'[37]

e. The comfort and the mystery of God's sovereignty (3:34–39)[38]

Still searching for a theology to undergird the return of his hope, the Man moves on from considering the prime reality of YHWH's compassion, faithfulness and mercy (22–24, 31–33) to his justice (34–36) and his sovereignty (37–39).[39]

Even if one must interpret the Babylonian invasion, the capture of Jerusalem and the exile of the people as constituting God's just judgment on people who had rebelled against him for generations (as the book's author and all the characters in it accept), nevertheless the events themselves were a gross violation of human dignity and rights. The implementing of God's justice had involved a bloody mass of human injustice. Surely God would not overlook that?

Each of verses 34–36 begins with an infinitive construct, pinpointing a dimension of injustice that the Man sees only too luridly illustrated in

---

[36] Parry, p. 106; italics original.

[37] O'Connor, p. 51.

[38] The precise syntax and exegesis of the terse and somewhat enigmatic sentences and questions in these verses are complex and debated. For an outline of all the issues involved, and an outstandingly clear account of the various options and interpretations offered by scholars, see Parry, pp. 106–113. In my view, the translations provided in the NIV, NRSV and ESV make legitimate sense, grammatically and theologically, of the whole passage.

[39] 'Verses 31–39 may be interpreted as a wave of thoughts and emotions: the poet knows that God will not cast off his people (represented by his person) for ever. He knows that God certainly sees what is wrong; but on the other hand, he knows that his suffering is well deserved' (Lalleman, p. 359).

what has happened to Jerusalem – though they are generic enough to apply to the length and breadth of human history. The NRSV captures the sense well:

> When all the prisoners of the land
>> are crushed under foot,
> when human rights are perverted
>> in the presence of the Most High,
> when one's case is subverted
>> – does the Lord not see it?[40]
> (34–36)

The answer to that final rhetorical question is, 'Yes, of course, God does see and God will deal with such injustices and put them all to rights.' That can bring some measure of comfort. The Judge of all the earth can be trusted to do justice (Gen. 18:25). That is an assumption that will govern the final prayer of the chapter (64–66). Let God deal with Israel's enemies as they had dealt with Israel.

But can the Man not see the tragic irony in what he has just said? Those things that Jerusalem has suffered at the hands of her enemies are the very same things that the prophets had accused Israel of doing repeatedly. Verses 34–36 could have been written by Amos. Generation after generation of Israelites had trampled on the rights of the poor and needy – and done it 'in the presence of the Most High'. And he had most assuredly *seen* it all – 'I have been watching! declares the LORD' (Jer. 7:11). It was the rock-hard truth of verses 34–36 that had brought Judah to where it was now – shattered by the God of justice.

But YHWH the God of all justice is also the only God there is. Where else is there to turn, then, whether for explanation or for hope? The sole

---

[40] I think this rhetorical question is the correct understanding of the final line of v. 36. The Hebrew simply reads, 'The Lord does not see.' If that is taken as a statement, then the Poet has swung back to a more accusatory stance, alongside Lady Zion who has appealed (apparently without success) to God to look and see what has happened to her. He would be speaking again like Job (cf. Job 24:1–12). O'Connor reads it that way ('the God of Lamentations is a blind God', p. 52). But that does not seem to fit the mood of these immediate verses with their apparent intention of advising hopeful submission to God and trust in his character. Some commentators keep it as a statement, but understand 'see' as 'approve' – 'the Lord does not approve' (ESV). But this is an otherwise unattested meaning of *rā'â*, and somewhat states the obvious. I follow those who read the line as a rhetorical question, 'Does the Lord not see?', with the intended answer, 'Yes, indeed he does. He will eventually redress such injustices.' I also think that 'does' is better than 'would' (NIV). The Man is not talking about hypothetical injustices and postulating that God *would* see them if they were to occur. He is thinking about the actual existing present evils of his own world – and (we might add) of ours.

sovereignty of YHWH constitutes the Man's final theological affirmation (37–39). But it is an affirmation couched in questions (each of the three verses is a question), which feels somehow appropriate since the uncompromising monotheism of this Old Testament poet pushes us out to and beyond the edges of our understanding.

Only the God who spoke creation into existence has the power to *speak and have it happen* (37; Ps. 33:6–9). God's will stands sovereignly behind all that takes place. So whatever power Nebuchadnezzar had exercised in carrying out his own devastating plans ultimately derived from the decree of God himself. God's plans trump the plans of nations (Ps. 33:10–11).

But, inasmuch as the events unleashed by Nebuchadnezzar were evil in the extreme, involving violence, destruction, cruelty and death, such events must also flow from the hand of God in some sense (38). Nebuchadnezzar's actions were the means by which the will of God for the punishment of his people was accomplished. Radical monotheism allows no other option. The Babylonians (like the Assyrians before them) might praise their own gods. But as Isaiah would robustly say, those gods are 'nothings'. Only the will of YHWH is sovereign in the governance of history. This produces the uncomfortable conclusion of verse 38. Once again it takes the form of a rhetorical question:

Is it not from the mouth of the Most High
that both calamities and good things come?

The answer clearly expected is 'Yes', but not with the implication that God is himself the ultimate source of evil per se. Interestingly, in Hebrew 'evils' is plural, whereas 'good' is singular. If there is any significance in this, it may imply that God is the source of all good (generic singular), and indeed 'evil things/events' are the product of his will when he acts in judgment. Suffering, defeat in battle, death and destruction are evil things, *calamities*. And if they are caused by human enemies who (whether they know it or not) are carrying out the judgment of God, then, yes, they come *from the mouth of* God – he has threatened them, warned about them, and finally unleashed them through the hands of fallen human beings. But the evil that was there in the first place – the evil of sin, disobedience and rebellion – has not come from God. Where it *did* come from (the ultimate origin of evil) is something the Bible never reveals to us. That remains a mystery. Evil is not there to be understood and explained, but to be resisted and ultimately destroyed.[41]

Nevertheless, the sovereignty of God behind all that is experienced in life is a truth that the Man affirms, along with the psalmists (Ps. 115:3), prophets (Amos 3:6; Isa. 45:7) and wise men (Job 2:10; Prov. 16:33) of Israel.

Now without further qualification, that assumption could produce a kind of resigned fatalism. But the next verse keeps us rooted in the moral framework of Israel's covenant faith. Given the sovereignty of God, the Man repeats ('naming' himself once more as the *geber* of v. 1 in v. 39; see ESV), who can *complain*? But he does not mean, 'Don't complain about anything. God's in charge. Whatever happens, happens. Get over it.' He has not lost his awareness of the fact that the terrible suffering he has witnessed is the result of sin reaping its own reward. *That* is what nobody can complain about (39).

3. Hope weeping: The Man leads his people's confession (3:40–51)

Once again the last word of the last line of a stanza triggers a sudden shift in the mood and direction of the poem. The last word of verse 39 is 'sins'. That's where the deepest problem lies. Whether or not God's reaction to their sin, at the hands of the Babylonians, has been excessive in the suffering and devastation it has caused (and there is plenty in the rest of the chapter and the book to suggest that the author still feels that it has been), the fact remains that sin is at the root of the disaster. Confession, then, not complaint, is the most needed immediate response.

So the Man calls for such confession, in words that echo Hosea (Hos. 6:1–3), Joel (Joel 2:12–14) and Jeremiah (if indeed it is not himself; Jer. 3:21 – 4:2; 14:7). The Man identifies himself with the people. He is not exhorting them to confess while he stands to one side. He is leading from the front. The corporate 'we' and 'us' of these verses echoes the confession prayer of Daniel 9, though it does not last as long, but breaks down in renewed lament.

His appeal is passionate, sincere and searching (40–41). There must be deep self-examination. Those who had been commanded to walk in the

---

[41] For further discussion of this vexing issue, see Christopher J. H. Wright, *The God I Don't Understand* (Grand Rapids: Zondervan, 2008).

ways of the Lord while they were still in the loins of Abraham (Gen. 18:19) must acknowledge that they had walked in their own *ways* – wandering ways that had taken them far from him. So they needed to *return to the* LORD – in a true repentance that Jeremiah had pleaded for to no avail for decades. Their prayers must be lifted up, like their hearts and hands, *to God in heaven* – even though a few verses earlier the complaint had been that no prayers could get through (8), a feeling that comes back soon (44)! But confession of sin will surely reach God, will it not?

Let them say it then, straight out, blunt and simple, all together now:

We [emphatically stressed as the opening word], *we have sinned and rebelled*

But then comes the shock:

and you [equally emphatic], *you have not forgiven.*
(42)

What has happened to the love, compassion, faithfulness and mercy of God, filling the air like incense a few moments ago? Is the Man faltering in his faith in the character of God? Worse, is he denying a fundamental element of biblical faith – namely that genuine repentance always meets with God's forgiveness? Some commentators think the Man has reached such a depth of negativity in his appalling suffering that he does indeed accuse God of breaking his own promise. Kathleen O'Connor paraphrases these verses: 'We did our part . . . we have turned to you, we have confessed our sins, but you have let us down.'[42] Adele Berlin puts it even more starkly.

But then, like a sudden jolt, comes v. 42, which starkly juxtaposes (without any grammatical conjunction) the admission of the people's sin with God's refusal to forgive . . . [Along with vv. 43–44] it is a fierce indictment of God. Nowhere in Lamentations, and perhaps in the entire Bible, is God's refusal to be present more strongly expressed. This is the climax of the poem's theodicy, for at this point the poet reaches a theological impasse.[43]

---

[42] O'Connor, p. 53.
[43] Berlin, p. 96.

Verse 42 is certainly theologically disturbing, and it does trigger a catalogue of the continuing inaccessibility of God and suffering of the people, as the *felt experience* of being not-yet-forgiven (43–47). But it is not necessary to read into it such a fundamental contradiction of God's own character and ways. Consider a number of points.

- This is only the start of the call to prayer and confession. The people have not in fact yet done what the Man urges them to do. Verse 42 states what the Man tells the people (including himself) to say to God. There is no actual act of repentance recorded as yet.

- Strictly speaking, the people so far only state the fact of their sin, not their turning away from it back to God. As Parry points out, they do not say, 'We have repented and turned back to you, and you have not forgiven.' They say, 'We have sinned and rebelled.' That was their present condition. It is good that they have acknowledged it at last, but it had been the reality for centuries. The language of repentance (return), and the prayer for God to grant it, does not come till the penultimate verse of the book (5:21).

- The verb *you have not forgiven* is a simple perfect. It may be a simple past tense: 'you *did not* forgive'. That is to say, the point is not that God is *now at this moment of their confession* refusing to respond with forgiveness (as the English perfect tense 'you have not forgiven' suggests), but that God *did* not forgive all the sin and rebellion of the past. He did not and could not simply overlook it, but finally acted in punitive judgment. The implication then is: 'We sinned and rebelled; you did not forgive.' That is, you did not let the guilty go unpunished, as you warned, and this disaster is the proof. This interpretation would be consistent with the way God told Jeremiah more than once to stop praying for the people, because they had sinned so unrepentantly and for so long that God's judgment had become inevitable and inescapable (Jer. 7:16; 11:14).

- The poetry of Lamentations comes out of the vortex of the disaster. It may have been written very soon after the fall of Jerusalem, perhaps while the city was still smouldering and the survivors were being chained up for their long march into exile. For as long as the realities of judgment and exile were present, it was theologically correct to say that God had not yet forgiven.[44] 'He . . . notes that YHWH is still angry and is still punishing Judah, and so has clearly not forgiven them yet. Forgiveness was conceived of very concretely – for God to forgive would be for the situation to change, and clearly that has not yet happened.'[45] It *would* happen, however. And prophets would declare the reality of God's forgiving grace (e.g. Isa. 43:25). But in the immediate aftermath of 587 BC, a sinful and rebellious people lived in a state of 'not-yet-forgiven-ness', though now excruciatingly conscious of what that meant.

What that meant was the absence of God (43–44) and the presence of their enemies (45–46) – both alike terrifying and humiliating.

Verses 43 and 44 each begin with God 'covering himself' – *with anger* (43), and *with a cloud* (44). Adele Berlin observes that both covering and cloud were powerful symbols of God's forgiving and protecting presence. The ark of the covenant had a 'covering' where God provided atonement. The cloud was God's guiding pillar, and had filled the tabernacle and temple to assure the people of his presence in their midst.[46] The Man has taken such massive traditional symbols and inverted them. Anger has replaced atonement. Absence has replaced gracious presence. The cloud that had protected Israel from their enemies now 'protects' God from Israel's prayers – *so that no prayer can get through*. Again, does the Man perceive the irony of his words? These words are uttered *in a prayer*, which surely (as he will later testify) must eventually be heard (56). God's resistance to his people's prayers is apparently not as impenetrable as he thought.

If God's ears are closed, their enemies' *mouths* are *wide* open – in mockery (46). The humiliation of Israel among the nations was a major part of their judgment (45). Ezekiel would later perceive that by inflicting such damage on the reputation of his people, YHWH had inflicted terrible damage on his own. And for that reason, for the sake of his own name, God would restore them (Ezek. 36:16–32). But that day is a long way ahead. The Man sees nothing but engulfing suffering and grief.

---

[44] Some New Testament theologians argue that even in Jesus' time, Jews had a feeling that the exile was not yet ended, even though physically they were back in the land. Forgiveness was still pending, and would only be experienced when the people were free from their oppressors again.

[45] Parry, p. 116.

[46] Berlin, p. 96.

Verse 47 says it all. Its stunning assonance in Hebrew is difficult to reproduce in English.

Paḥad and *paḥat* have happened to us, *haššē't* and *haššāber.*

The ESV makes a good attempt with alliteration at least:

Panic and pitfall have come upon us,
    devastation and destruction.

And so the strong Man, the *geber*, dissolves in floods of tears (48–49). Echoing the weeping prophet (or speaking as he himself had done many times before), he has become a fountain, a torrent of tears. He joins Lady Zion in grief. In fact, it seems he remembers her again, sitting silently since the end of chapter 2. For just as the Poet had told *her* to weep without ceasing (2:18–19), and just as she had pleaded with God to look down and see, so now the Man says *he* will weep until God does just that (50). However long it takes, he will give God no rest. His tears will flow *until the LORD looks down from heaven and sees.* There is surely an implied assumption that in the end God will, God must. Israel's history, Israel's Scriptures, and even the Poet's rhetoric (34–36) affirm that YHWH is the God who sees – to which the Man will shortly add his own testimony (55–59).

For the moment, however, the weeping continues, for God's eyes seem closed to what the Man's eyes see, which *brings grief to my soul* – namely the terrible suffering of *all the women of my city* (51). The double *my soul . . . my city* adds to the personal poignancy of his pain. *Women* is 'daughters of my city'. That could mean the literal fate of the women, already painfully described in chapters 1 and 2. Or it could refer to the destruction of the towns and villages of Judah – daughters of the capital city. The poetic ambiguity allows for both, for both brought overflowing grief.

4. Hope pleading: The Man encourages his people's trust (3:52–66)

In this final section of the chapter, the Man speaks again in the first person as he had done in the earlier part of the chapter. But there is a significant change of mood, in the wake of the central affirmations and call to confession. He returns to the terrible dangers that he has endured, and still does, but gone are the barely concealed accusations against God himself. 'He' is no longer the one inflicting the suffering (1–18). Rather, God has become the only one who can rescue him from his enemies. God is no longer portrayed as the enemy, but as the champion defender and redeemer. You can vent your anger and grief at him, but in the end you have to trust him. There is no other.

The sudden shift from lament to testimony may seem confusing. If the reality of the situation is as it is described in verses 42–47 (continuing suffering in a state of being not-yet-forgiven and certainly not yet delivered), then what is all this talk of rescue and redemption about in verses 56–58?

I find Robin Parry's interpretation once again convincing.[47] We must remember that the Man is speaking *both as an individual* who has experienced all that has befallen the city, *and also as a personification* of the city itself. The 'I' of the poem can oscillate between personal and corporate reference. That is what seems to happen here.

In verses 52–58, the Man appears to be describing a personal experience in his own past life of being delivered by God from terrifying and life-threatening danger. God heard his prayer, took up his case, and redeemed his life. He then offers this as an encouragement to his personified self, speaking from verse 59 onwards as the city. The people (his corporate self) can trust God to vindicate them against their enemies, because God has done that in his own lived experience and memory (his personal self).

Verses 52–54 describe some situation of acute danger that the Man has gone through: physical assault with intent to kill. Now the language could of course be metaphorical. The psalmists could freely use pictures of being thrown into a pit, or attacked by wild beasts, or drowning, as vivid metaphors for being falsely accused or being the victim of a lethal conspiracy (e.g. Pss 22:12–21; 40:2; 88:6–7; 116:3). But among those to whom such things actually happened quite literally were Joseph and, of course, Jeremiah. In fact, it is hard to read these verses without imagining that the author either clearly had Jeremiah 38 in mind, or was Jeremiah himself.

---

[47] 'I propose that the *geber* is still the speaker and that he is still speaking to his fellow sufferers in Jerusalem. Here, as throughout the poem, his trials are to be taken as a microcosm of their own trials . . . His story is intimately connected to [Jerusalem's], and it is precisely this fact which is the rationale behind the final section. I propose that the man tells his story as an encouragement to his fellow sufferers in Jerusalem' (Parry, p. 119). The same interpretation is adopted by Re'emi, pp. 113–115, and House, pp. 425–427.

The cistern that Jeremiah was thrown into had no water, but Jeremiah sank down into the watery slime, which would have made it impossible to lie down without danger of death by drowning. The suffocating trapped terror of such a nightmare screams out in verse 54. 'I said, "I am finished!"' The words are in direct speech, not the slightly inadequate *I thought I was about to perish* (NIV). The Man is recounting a moment when he faced certain death.

But verses 55–59 follow the familiar path of salvation psalms: *I called . . . you heard . . . you came . . . you redeemed.* The God who at this present moment in Jerusalem seems so far away, unhearing, unseeing (43–44), at that remembered time in the past *had* heard and *did* come near. And when the Man had spoken what he thought were his last words, God spoke the only divine words recorded in this book. But they were the only words the Man needed to hear back then, and Jerusalem needs to hear now.

> I said, 'I am finished!'
> You said, 'Do not fear.'

God answered the prayer. God did for the Man what Job longed for God to do for him (and trusted that he would): *You, Lord, took up my case; you redeemed my life* (58). Jeremiah was indeed rescued from the pit, though it was not the end of his sufferings.

Thus far, the Man's personal testimony.

Now (from v. 59), he speaks as the city. He takes up the complaint of Lady Zion at the end of chapter 1 and makes it his own. He appeals to God to *uphold my cause* – that is, to come back and take the side of Jerusalem against the enemies who have so viciously and destructively conspired against her (60–63). And finally he repeats and amplifies Lady Zion's call for God to take vengeance on those who have so cruelly treated her (64–66; cf. 1:21c–22).

Such requests and the vivid language in which they are framed are characteristic of Jeremiah and some psalms. Behind them lies the same assumption as in verses 34–36. God does not and cannot ignore the evil deeds of the persistently unrepentant wicked who trample on others. The justice with which God will redeem and vindicate those who call out to him, especially those who do so with honest confession of sin and repentance, is the same justice with which he will ultimately *destroy* those who refuse to do so. The whole earth – all that lies *under the heavens of the*

LORD (66) – will one day be cleansed from all evil and evildoers. Such is the promise of the New as well as the Old Testament.

Reflections

1. What difference does it make to your former appreciation of a hymn like 'Great Is Thy Faithfulness', or a song like 'The Steadfast Love of the Lord Never Ceases', to have explored the context in which they come here in Lamentations 3?
2. Has your study of 3:31–33 affected or changed your understanding of the character of God?
3. Can a Christian pray the prayer of 3:61–66? If not, why not? And if so, in what circumstances and with what theological qualifications?

Lamentations 4:1–22

4. It is finished

'Êkâ! 'Alas!' cries the Poet again, reverting to the opening word of chapters 1 and 2 (and doubling it in 4:1 and 2). If we thought that the astonishing words of hope and assurance at the heart of chapter 3, or the testimony of some past experience of God's deliverance (3:52–58), might lead to a 'happy ending', we are brought very sharply back to reality – the reality of a city in total devastation and a people in subhuman degradation. Chapter 4 returns to the horrors of the prolonged siege of Jerusalem and its awful climax when the Babylonians invaded the city, hunted down the people and captured King Zedekiah. Whereas 2:1–9 featured mainly the levelling of the physical structures of the city, chapter 4 focuses on the levelling of the people – all alike and all together reduced to the same depths of extreme deprivation.

So the suffering is by no means over, and nor is the account of it. Hope may lie in the future, but the present is unrelieved agony – and it must be voiced and heard. Lament is not yet exhausted.

The one who is lamenting, however, may be approaching exhaustion. In chapter 4 the intensity of the anger, protest, hope and theological wrestling of chapter 3 is left behind. We hear no more dialogue between the Poet and Lady Zion, no more poignant appeals from her to the Lord. And the abundant imagery of the triple-line stanzas of chapters 1 and 2 is shortened to two-line descriptions that are more stark and economical in their brush-strokes. The reality is just as horrific as ever, but the effort of expressing it seems more and more beyond the power of words – even poetic words with the continued art and craft of the acrostic form.[1] The

---

[1] Kathleen O'Connor says of ch. 4, 'Its two speakers, an unidentified narrator and the people, appear exhausted and hopeless . . . stunned and depleted . . . Resignation and despair have triumphed over anger and resistance' (pp. 58–59).

Poet, like his book of poems itself, is limping ever more weakly to a stand-still. Only a single line at the very end of the chapter sustains a slender thread of hope (22a) – a slender thread from which will dangle the even shorter communal prayer of chapter 5, where the skill and effort of acrostic composition is abandoned altogether.

The structure of the chapter is straightforward.

- 1–10: The Poet describes the devastating effect of the siege on every section of society.
- 11–16: He singles out particularly the sin and the fate of the leaders.
- 17–20: It seems that all hope from any quarter is gone.
- 21–22: A prophetic oracle envisages the doom of Edom, and the ending of Judah's exile.

1. The degradation of a whole population (4:1–10)

Shocking reversal is the unrelenting drumbeat of this chapter from begin-ning to end:

- What was precious is treated as worthless.
- Children who should be nurtured are being starved.
- The rich are reduced to the rubbish heap.
- Sumptuous colours are turned to black.
- Ruddy good health has shrunk and shrivelled.
- Mothers who should feed their children are eating them instead.
- Holy men have become dirty and defiled.
- The royal protector of life is himself trapped in a pit.
- But . . . the gloating enemy and the suffering Jerusalem will also change places.

The whole community from top to bottom – from the elders to the infants, from the king in his palace to the mother in her kitchen – has been turned upside down and shaken out, and left shattered and scattered like trash littering the streets. Such was the effect of the prolonged siege and the final invasion of the city – both of which are portrayed here in all their horror. 'The picture is . . . of the abrogation of all that was normal in Judean society, a drastic reversal of fortunes, socially and physically, caused by the ravages of wartime famine ... all human dignity has been lost.'[2]

a. Gold turned to clay (4:1–2)

Nothing is more valuable than *gold*, other than the word of God himself (Ps. 19:10);[3] nothing more precious than the 'holy stones' that adorned the temple and the high priest's breastplate. But now the gold has *lost its lustre*[4] and the *sacred gems* are scattered like worthless pebbles that are trodden underfoot on every street. The combination of gold and 'holy stones' may well have a literal point of reference in the destruction of the temple and all its vessels and ornaments. The picture would still be metaphorical, though, since it is unlikely that the rapacious Babylonians would have squandered the valuable loot by scattering it on the streets.

The parallelism with verse 2, however, shows us that, even if valuable temple artefacts are in mind in verse 1, the primary significance of the metaphor is the people themselves – *the precious children of Zion.*[5] They are the ones who, though *worth their weight in gold*, are being treated like broken pottery, thrown out as worthless *pots of clay* – fragile, broken, despised. A whole population is being literally trashed.

Another irony in this reversal comes in the last words of verse 2 – *the work of a potter's hands.* In the thrust of the metaphor, of course, this functions as the opposite of the gold and gems. Precious metal and stones, the jewels of God's own creation, have mutated into mere human artefacts. But that phrase was also a way of describing Israel itself. As God had done for the first human being (Gen. 2:7), so he had done for Israel – fashioning them with the loving care of a potter shaping the clay. That was a way of describing the covenant relationship when Israel needed to appeal to God for fatherly compassion.

---

[2] Berlin, p. 103.

[3] Three different words for *gold* are used in vv. 1–2, emphasizing its uniqueness and value.

[4] It has been pointed out that, strictly speaking, pure gold does not corrode or lose its shine. That being so (and doubtless the ancient author was as much aware of it as a modern metallurgist), the 'impossible' metaphor may in itself be hinting at the shockingly impossible nature of what had happened to Judah and Jerusalem.

[5] Probably the phrase in v. 2, (lit.) 'sons of Zion', does not refer to young children (who do become the focal point in vv. 3–4 and 10), but rather indicates all the citizens of Jerusalem, in the same way that the comparable phrase 'the children of Israel' does not mean the youngsters only, but the whole people of Israel. V. 2 is making the general, 'headline' point that the whole human community of Zion has been transformed from being like precious gold and gems to being trodden underfoot like worthless pottery. The rest of the chapter will illustrate that fact in more detail.

Yet you, LORD, are our Father.
  We are the clay, you are the potter;
  we are all *the work of your hand.*
(Isa. 64:8; my italics)

But here, a metaphor that could be used to convey the preciousness of Israel in God's hands has been subverted into a picture of their apparent worthlessness under God's judgment.

The tragedy of something very precious being squandered as though worthless is an echo of Jeremiah 2. Jeremiah lists the amazing privileges that Israel had enjoyed in their relationship with God (the love of a 'husband', redemption from slavery, protection in the wilderness, the gift of the land with all its fruitfulness – a rich inheritance indeed), but instead 'they followed worthless idols and became worthless themselves' (Jer. 2:5). Now, almost a generation after Jeremiah first uttered that perceptive assessment, they are being treated as befits the worthlessness to which they have sunk.

There is a sober warning here for God's people in any generation. When we fail to hold on to the gold and sacred stones of what we have and what we are in Christ, and fail to live in accordance with that status and story, then we are in danger of becoming worthless to God and indeed to God's world and God's mission.

b. Children left to starve (4:3–4)

Jackals were associated with ruined cities (as in 5:18) and with the howling of people in deep grief (Job 30:29; Isa. 34:13; Mic. 1:8). For that reason, reference to jackals would be wholly appropriate for the situation of both city and people in the cataclysm of 587 BC. However, in an inversion of their usual metaphoric significance, jackals are here pictured as models of motherly care – in the simple act of suckling their young. But in stark contrast to the instinctive caring behaviour of despised wild creatures, Israel's mothers have become *heartless*. The word *my people* is (Heb.) 'the daughter – my people', hinting that women are particularly in view. The animal imagery is startling. Judah's mothers are no longer caring (like jackals!), but cruel (*like ostriches!*). Ostriches were thought to abandon their eggs and their young,[6] and (whether or not the proverbial belief

---

[6] Job 39:13–17 provides a rather amusing picture of ostrich behaviour.

matches biological fact) mothers in Jerusalem were forced to such un-
natural behaviour by the extremities of the siege.

It is as hard to read verse 4 without tears as it is to watch modern
examples of exactly what it describes on our TV screens, in situations of
drought, famine and war. The suffering of children is surely one of the
most diabolical outcomes of evil and violence.

Thirst and hunger stalk the city under siege. Infants clinging to
starving mothers find no nourishment at the breast. If *the infant's tongue
sticks to the roof of its mouth*, that may indeed be *because of thirst*. But
on other occasions when that phrase occurs, it refers to the inability to
utter a sound (Ps. 137:6; Ezek. 3:26). The painful image is of a pathetic
emaciated baby, too weak either to suck or even to cry. If anything is
harder to bear than a child crying (for good reason), it is a child wasted,
wretched and weak beyond even the ability to cry. Meanwhile, children
needing solid food *beg for bread, but no one gives it to them* – and we are
left to imagine whether that was because there was no bread left for
anybody to share, or because those who had some were too desperate in
their own extremity of hunger to share it with starving children.
Humanity itself is perishing.[7]

c. The wealthy forced to scavenge (4:5–6)

Whatever modern tastes may think about the health benefits (or the
opposite) of rich foods and *delicacies*, they were counted in Israel as
among the particular blessings of God (Gen. 49:20), even if they were not
universally shared. But in the terrible levelling power of hunger in the
siege, those who had once enjoyed such blessings are to be found *destitute
in the streets* along with those for whom the streets might have been their
only home – beggars and outcasts.

Along with good food goes good clothing, as the lifestyle of those with
privileged birth and upbringing. But what value does your bulging
wardrobe have when you are starving? You can't eat cloth. So even
those who had the most expensive clothing of that day (*purple*, or
scarlet)[8] joined the rest of the scavenging population in 'the democracy of

---

[7] Kathleen O'Connor speaks of 'the tragedy of the children, sharp as sketches engraved on stone.
Children are starving, and their lives fade away. Mothers live in excruciating pain as their breasts dry up and
food supplies disappear' (p. 61).

[8] This deep colour was the most expensive fast dye in the ancient world, and therefore only the wealthiest
(or the most politically prominent) could afford clothing of that colour. Lydia, as a trader in purple cloth (Acts
16:13–15), was therefore a businesswoman of substantial means.

deprivation'.[9] They *now lie on ash heaps.* Literally, they 'embrace', or 'cling to' (ESV, NRSV), ash heaps. Whether this is in a desperate search for scraps of food among the garbage, or because they have been driven from human society with contagious ill-health (8), like Job, they are now no better off than the poorest beggar in the land. Hunger reverses the redemptive direction of God's characteristic action, which is to lift the poor out of the ashes (1 Sam. 2:8; Ps. 113:7). But when hunger is the by-product of God's judgment working through human aggression, then the rich find no protection in their luxurious food and finery.

What was the worst example of God's judgment that an Israelite could think of? Sodom and Gomorrah would come quickly to mind. Those cities stand in the whole Bible as the proverbial prototype of the wrath of God against arrogant human wickedness.[10] But at least their judgment had been quick! As his mind's eye recalls the appalling prolonged suffering of his people, the Poet comes to a poisoned comparison: the suffering of Jerusalem has been even *greater than that of Sodom* (6).

What he actually says is, 'The transgression (*'āwōn*) of my people is greater than the sin (*ḥaṭṭā't*) of Sodom.' There is some ambiguity here, which may well be intentional. The two words can simply mean transgression and sin, but they can sometimes be used to mean the *punishment* that transgression and sin inevitably bring. Most likely the Poet's main point here is that the punishment of Jerusalem *because of their sin* is greater than that of Sodom *because of theirs* – the point being that for Sodom it was sudden and direct from the hand of God, whereas for Jerusalem it was long and drawn out at the hand of human enemies.[11] However, given that some prophets could indeed accuse Judah of being as wicked as, and even more wicked than, Sodom (Isa. 1:9–10; Ezek. 16:46–52), the words may have a more direct meaning too. If Jerusalem's punishment was worse

---

[9] O'Connor, p. 61.

[10] The sin of Sodom accumulates through the references in the Old Testament. At first we read that there is an 'outcry' from there (Gen. 18:20–21) – the term used to describe social oppression and cruelty (as of the Hebrews in Egypt). Then we read of the violent attempted rape by the men of Sodom of the two men who had come to Lot's house (Gen. 19). Sodom is also a place of perverted and aggressive sexual abuse. Isaiah compares Jerusalem to Sodom (Isa. 1:9–10), and goes on to speak of the political corruption, injustice and bloodshed that justified the comparison. Ezekiel is the most concise: 'This was the sin of your sister Sodom: she and her daughters were arrogant, overfed and unconcerned; they did not help the poor and needy. They were haughty and did detestable things before me' (Ezek. 16:49–50). The catalogue is shockingly modern. Oppression of the poor, sexual perversion and violence, corruption, bloodshed, arrogance, affluence, consumerism and callousness. We (especially in the West) are still living in Sodom.

[11] Probably the last line of v. 6 should be translated, not as 'without a hand turned *to help her*' (NIV), but as 'without a hand raised *against her*' – i.e. against Sodom. They did not have to endure the cruelty of human hands, but simply suffered quick and immediate destruction by God through natural elements.

than Sodom's, then so was her sin – a point that will be explicit in the second section of the poem.

Jesus knew and used this stinging comparison with Sodom (Matt. 11:23–24). No doubt it was as offensive to the citizenry of Capernaum as it was to Jerusalem or the exiles in the mouth of Isaiah or Ezekiel. But the point is very sobering. The wicked stand universally under the wrath of God against all that is evil. And evil is evil anywhere. Nevertheless, God's judgment is discriminating, and those who sin, resist and rebel against the full knowledge and experience of his revelation, love and grace will be treated (according to Jesus) with far greater severity than those who have had no such privilege. Jerusalem's sin and Jerusalem's punishment were greater even than Sodom's. The comparison in Lamentations 4:6 is doubtless intended for poetic and rhetorical effect. But it contains a theological principle that is soberly endorsed in the New Testament, for our warning.

d. The healthy shrunk to skin and bone (4:7–9)

Along with good food and good clothing, good health is one of the benefits of wealth. Or more accurately (since the wealthy can subject themselves to very unhealthy lifestyles), ill-health frequently accompanies acute poverty. Our Poet here pictures those whose position in society (*princes*) had afforded them the time, wealth and luxury to look after their physical bodies. So they used to glow and shine in pampered splendour. Their skin had been healthily pale (not sunburnt like peasants or slaves). Their complexion had been healthily rosy like *rubies*.[12] Their hair (perhaps, or just their general form) had been healthily shiny like dark blue *lapis lazuli*. They were, in short, 'a picture of ruddy good health',[13] models of the handsome sort of man a girl could fall in love with (Song 5:10–16).

But now (8)?

Now you wouldn't even know them if you bumped into them *in the streets* (8a) – no matter how exalted, famous and recognizable they had once been. Hunger has done to them what it has done to everybody. It has drained their colour and shrivelled their skin. Their rainbow of good health has turned to the blackness of night.[14] They are starved and

---

[12] Like David's: 1 Sam. 16:12; 17:42.

[13] Berlin, p. 108.

[14] Adele Berlin notes the poetic and effective use of colour in this poem. 'In fact, color is one of the striking features of the chapter: gold and scarlet (vv. 1, 2, 5), white, red, sapphire, black (vv. 7, 8). Bright colors represent the earlier conditions; as the famine progresses, the colors are erased from the picture, and all that

dehydrated. The 'beautiful people' have joined the ranks of the desperate masses they once ruled. Neither wealth nor health survives the ravages of starvation by siege.

Watching that slow shrinking of a sleek and healthy human body to a blackened, shrivelled, scavenging skeleton produces another poisoned comparison (9). There are better ways to die. The language of verse 9 is powerful. The verse begins with the Hebrew word 'good'. What can possibly be 'good' in this litany of suffering? Only one thing would be good – better, in fact. And that would be to die quickly rather than to die slowly. A sword and hunger can both kill you, and the same word is used for both (which the NIV somewhat obscures). But *the sword* is better. *Hunger* is just another way to 'bleed' to death, only very slowly.[15] 'It is a sorry state, though, when death by a sword is considered a mercy.'[16] Adele Berlin captures the sense well:

> Better off were those slain by the sword
>> than those slain by famine,
> who bleed slowly, stabbed by the lack
>> of produce from the field.[17]

e. The caring turned to cannibals (4:10)

The Poet simply cannot get the children out of his mind. Their suffering has drawn his anguished sympathy repeatedly (1:11, 18; 2:11–12, 19, 20). Now again he forces himself and us to picture the ultimate extremity of the siege: children are not just being neglected by being given no food (4), they are being *cooked* for food themselves. The horror recalls Lady Zion's appalled protest to the very heavens at such a thing (2:20).

There have been many reversals in his survey so far, but this is the worst, and his language makes it painfully stark. For who is doing this inconceivably cruel deed? *Compassionate women*! The very word in Hebrew contains the essence of motherhood – the womb. The clash of

---

remains is dullness and blackness' (pp. 103–104). She also suggests that the blackness may possibly indicate an outbreak of bubonic plague, which is characterized by blackened skin caused by subcutaneous bleeding – hence the common term for it, 'the Black Death' (*idem*, p. 109).

[15] *They waste away* is literally 'they flow' – probably an allusion to bleeding, but here the startling metaphor is that starving people are 'bleeding' from lack of the produce of the fields.

[16] Longman III, p. 382.

[17] Berlin, p. 99. Cf. other attempts to capture the parallel phrases: 'victims of the sword ... victims of hunger' (ESV); 'pierced by the sword ... pierced by hunger' (NRSV).

images breaks the limits of imagination: that the child of a mother's womb could be the object of both a mother's care and a mother's cooking.[18]

And that such a thing should be done among *my people* (10b)! This is the third time that this phrase has been used in this first section of the chapter (cf. 3, 6). It is a rich and resonant term, which at one level shows the identification of the Poet with his own people. He is describing suffering that he has witnessed and shared. Even if Lady Zion is silent, the Poet speaks on her behalf – these are 'my people', just as she had spoken of 'my children' (1:16) and 'my young men and young women' (1:18; 2:21).

But at another level that single word in Hebrew, *my people*, has richly covenantal resonance too, since it was most often spoken by God himself (as we saw above at 2:11). Indeed, in Jeremiah it is often indistinguishable whether the word is uttered by the prophet or by God (amounting to the same thing, of course). So it is at least worth reflecting on how the words of the Poet here express the emotions of God – and in that sense virtually raise the poetic to the level of the prophetic. Even though the form is lament *to* God, it can be read with some justification as lament *by* God. 'My people are destroyed,' says *God*! Yes, we have been told that these horrors of Lamentations 4:1–10 are the outworking of God's judgment executed through the hands of evil men. But God cannot look on the suffering of his own people, even under judgment, without the pangs of covenant memory: these wretched, scavenging, starving, dehumanized living dead – these are *my people*. The Poet's emotions are God's too, just as the prophet's tears flowed from God's heart, just as the Messiah's tears would flow for the suffering of Jerusalem in a later century, once more brought upon themselves by their resistance to the embracing motherly love of their covenant God (Luke 13:34–35; 19:41–44).

2. The defilement of 'holy' leaders (4:11–16)

a. The unthinkable (4:11–12)

If there is a hint of divine grief in the 'my people' of verse 10, the emotion swings to divine anger in verse 11. Natural fire will raze any city to the ground. The fire of God's judgment is so supernaturally devouring that it

---

[18] As at 2:20, we cannot be certain whether children were killed to be eaten, or had already died and were then used for food (most likely the latter). As we pointed out there also, this was one of the curses listed in Deut. 28:53–57. This horror could be foreseen and predicted in such standard lists of curses precisely because it was a known reality in the extremities of hunger caused by the ruthlessness of siege warfare.

has *consumed* even the *foundations* of Zion. The Babylonian inferno was the physical reality, but the Poet knows the more terrifying spiritual force behind it. The wrath of Nebuchadnezzar was merely the instrument of the wrath of God.

There is irony, and possibly even a hint of hope, in the verb with which he begins verse 11: 'The Lord has *fully used up* his wrath.' The irony is that it is exactly the same verb that expressed the wonderful affirmation of 3:22 – that 'the Lord's compassions are *not* fully used up'. The sense is of expending something till it is utterly finished. So, in 3:22 we are assured that God's compassions can never be expended till they are used up – there will always be more, as infinite as God is eternal. In 4:11, however, the Lord *has* fully expended his anger – that is, he has poured it out in its fullest entirety; he *has given full vent to his wrath.*

Indeed so. But if God has 'fully used up' his anger in the cataclysm, might it then be so fully spent that there could be hope of grace and restoration ahead? It was certainly part of Israel's faith (and the Bible's teaching) that while God's mercy and compassion are eternal, his anger is not. 'You do not stay angry for ever,' said Micah (7:18). 'The Lord will not reject for ever,' the Poet himself has said (3:31, NRSV). Such a perspective must have been excruciatingly hard to cling to in a starving city set ablaze when the Lord *poured out his fierce anger.* But it does spark the glimmer of prophetic light at the end of this chapter's dark tunnel (22a).

Meanwhile, however, the event itself was unbelievably shocking (12). The Poet here engages in some poetic hyperbole and 'transference'. It is well known that the people of Israel, for generations, had believed that Jerusalem was inviolable. It was enshrined in their worship (Pss 46; 48; 125). They had taken the amazing deliverance of Jerusalem from the Assyrians in 701 BC, in accordance with the prophetic assurance of Isaiah at the time, and turned it into a perpetual guarantee. YHWH would *never* allow his city to be invaded or his temple to be destroyed, they firmly believed. That is why, when Jeremiah dared to say that God would indeed do just that, unless the people changed their ways, they accused him of blasphemous false prophecy and almost lynched him (Jer. 7 and 26). Such a prospect was simply unthinkable, and certainly unspeakable.

But here the Poet universalizes the shock. Nobody in the whole wide world could have imagined that Jerusalem would fall to invading enemies (12)![19] Poetic exaggeration, no doubt. But it does remind us that all God's actions in, for and against Israel in the Old Testament have a wider significance. Israel was called into existence for the sake of God's mission of blessing the nations. When God acted to redeem Israel, the nations knew about it and trembled (Exod. 15:14–16). When God acted to judge Israel, the nations would be amazed and ask questions (Deut. 29:24). And when God would in due course redeem Israel yet again, bringing them back from exile, it would be in the sight of the nations and for the purpose of vindicating YHWH's own name and reputation (Ezek. 36:22–23). For whether in judgment or ultimately in cosmic redemption, the will of God is to be known for who he is among all nations and throughout his whole creation. And the amazement of the nations will become the praise of the redeemed, and 'the earth will be filled with the knowledge of the glory of the LORD as the waters cover the sea' (Hab. 2:14).

b. The untouchable (4:13–16)

We met the *prophets* and *priests* before, and in the same close company as the despairing women and children. It was in Lady Zion's last speech at the end of chapter 2, when she challenged God about priests and prophets being slaughtered in the temple itself (2:20). Is this God's answer, through the Poet? Plenty of priestly and prophetic blood was shed in the temple when the Babylonians invaded. But was it innocent blood? Not at all. Rather, it was those religious officials (priests, prophets and *elders* also [16]) who were themselves guilty of shedding *the blood of the righteous* (13b).

Some commentators are reluctant to think that the accusation is meant literally – that some priests and prophets had been committing murder in the city. Perhaps 'shedding blood' is a metaphor for idolatry, as in Ezekiel 22:1–5, where it stands in parallel with 'becoming defiled by the idols you have made'.[20] Or perhaps it means that priests and prophets have condoned or acquiesced in the corruption and violence that characterized Jerusalem in the late monarchy – and thus shared the guilt of those who committed such sins. But it is hardly stretching imagination to believe that some religious officials had sunk to the same level, and indeed probably

---

[19] Similar shock waves rippled round the world when 9/11 brought the unthinkable to the USA – who could have believed that the financial centre of the world's superpower could be 'invaded' and brought to the dust by 'enemies and foes'?

[20] Though even there, the parallelism of the phrases need not mean that they both refer to the same thing (idolatry). It seems more likely that Ezekiel is referring to actual shedding of blood in Jerusalem alongside idolatrous rituals and many other social evils described in that searing chapter.

justified their violence with religious rationales. Jeremiah certainly experienced murderous intent and actual physical violence from the temple staff (Jer. 18:18; 20:1–2). And it was precisely the priests and prophets who instigated a mob lynching against Jeremiah in the temple itself, from which he was rescued only by the intervention of some village elders. And to prove the reality of such danger, we are told that another prophet (Uriah) had been murdered for saying the same things as Jeremiah (Jer. 26:7–8, 11, 16–19, 20–23).

Murderous clerics are murderous clerics in any age, and the church down the ages has been defaced by their crimes as much as, if not more than, Old Testament Israel. The Protestant Reformation and the Roman Catholic Counter-Reformation both had their quota of painful executions of those of opposing religious persuasion, carried out by men in 'holy orders'. There were known to be church pastors caught up in the crimes of genocide in Rwanda in 1994. A black South African friend has told me how much he struggled to retain his identity as an evangelical when, during imprisonment, he knew that among the interrogators and torturers of the state security forces were some who were elders in white evangelical churches. The potential for violence and murder lies deep in fallen human hearts, and simply attaining whatever status equates to 'priest and prophet' is no guarantee of innocence. Indeed, religion can be used to cloak and condone such acts. And in more recent times, we are shocked by the scale of sexual child abuse among clergy, which, even if it is not shedding of blood, has certainly wrecked and sullied the lives of many and driven them far from whatever gospel message the church might have brought them.

Verse 13 does not mean to lay the blame exclusively on these religious leaders. It is clear from the historical narrative and from Jeremiah's preaching that there was a breakdown in social morality throughout the whole community. Nevertheless, like Hosea before him, Jeremiah discerned and exposed the greater responsibility of those leaders who were supposed to restrain such evil, but instead allowed it to flourish (Hos. 4:1–9; Jer. 2:8; 5:4–5).

> From the least to the greatest,
>   all are greedy for gain;
> prophets and priests alike,
>   all practise deceit.
> (Jer. 6:13; cf. 8:7–12)

What then will be the specific destiny of these men who had been entrusted with the holy offices of priest and prophet, or community responsibility as elders? Verses 14–16 paint yet another terrible reversal – several in fact.

i. 'The seers cannot see' (4:14a)[21]

It is not just that these people, who had once lived in the exalted status of spiritual leadership in the nation, are now on the streets like everybody else. It is also that they *grope through the streets as if they were blind.* Those expected to see visions that would give guidance to others are unable to see in front of their own feet. 'Leaders who should see God's ways and God's visions are blind.'[22] That is a reality that has sadly never gone away. When leaders among God's own people, including today's global church, are corrupt, or negligent – neither teaching God's word nor living by it themselves – the whole church suffers the consequences while its leaders sink in growing disrepute.

ii. The holy people are defiled (4:14b)

Priests especially were holy – set apart for their service to God and his temple. They had to live as far as possible in a state of ritual purity. But now, the exposure of their blood-guilt makes them untouchable. Even their clothes, once symbolic of their status, are shunned as untouchable, for fear of defilement.

iii. Those who once decided the fate of leprosy sufferers are now treated as lepers themselves (4:15)

It was the unhappy lot of those who contracted contagious skin diseases to be quarantined from the community – 'They must live alone; they must live outside the camp.' And it was the priests who had to make that diagnosis and impose that sad destiny (Lev. 13:1–46).[23] But now, the priests themselves have become social pariahs, both among their own people and wherever they may wander. They are unwelcome everywhere (15). Somehow, those who have been accorded the greatest trust are treated with the greatest

---

[21] Parry, p. 139.

[22] O'Connor, p. 65.

[23] The symptoms described may not be leprosy (Hansen's disease, as known today), but various forms of flaky skin conditions. I use the word 'leper' in the heading fully aware that it is no longer an acceptable term for those suffering from the disease. It has become an ugly term of social abuse – and it is in that sense, as a metaphor that fits the social reality of v. 15, that it is used in the heading.

contempt and exclusion when they fall – like corrupt police officers, or sexually abusing teachers or doctors or entertainers, or paedophile priests. In the case of these priests and prophets, ritual purity is reversed to repulsive pollution. God's judgment is yet again executed through human behaviour. But human rejection is not the worst of their woes.

iv. Those who had lived in God's presence now find no respect on earth (4:16)

It is hard to capture the poignant wordplay of verse 16. The words *the* Lord *himself* are in Hebrew 'the face of the Lord', meaning his personal presence. The sense is that, whereas these people had once known (or claimed) close personal access to the presence of God in the course of their priestly and prophetic ministry, God has now *scattered them* from his presence altogether and *no longer watches over them*. Then the second line also begins with the word 'face' (Heb.): 'The face of the priests they do not lift up.' Those whom God no longer allows in his presence are soon denied *honour* and respect in the presence of the people. This is a precise example of the aphorism spoken to Eli (significantly in a context that portrays corrupt and greedy priests – Eli's own sons): 'Those who honour me I will honour, but those who despise me will be disdained' (1 Sam. 2:30). And not just despised in the church. The disgrace of leaders among God's people brings on them, and the church itself, the opprobrium of a watching world. Instead of being agents by which the world can be sanctified through repentance and faith, 'the failures of prophets and priests contaminate and make profane the entire world'.[24]

We might wonder at the harshness of all this. Is there no place for repentance, even by fallen leaders among God's people? Do we not extend the grace of forgiveness and restoration to disgraced pastors and Christian leaders? The answer surely is, Yes, when such repentance is deep and real and is met with appropriate forgiving grace and pastoral discipline. But that was not the position of the priests, prophets and elders here described. On the contrary, Jeremiah had pleaded with them *for forty years* to turn from their personal wickedness, and to lead the people in a change of ways. But for forty years they had refused such repentance and spurned the grace that could have followed. All that was left for them was the bleakness of judgment – by God and society.

---

24 O'Connor, p. 65.

3. The end has come (4:17–20)

At this point, the Poet shifts to the first person plural – 'we' and 'our'. He has witnessed what he describes – which is the final stage of the siege, the vain hopes of being rescued by Egypt (17), the breaching of the city (18) and capturing of the fleeing population (19), and the final capture of the king himself (20).

a. No salvation (4:17)

Almost certainly, Egypt is the *nation* in mind here. Judah had sought the help of Egypt in the past against Assyria – and been bitterly disappointed (Isa. 31:1–3; 36:4–6). Having learnt nothing, they hoped Egypt might help them against the Babylonians. At first, it seemed as if help was indeed coming – and the Babylonians briefly withdrew, giving a short lull in the siege. But it was all *in vain*. The Egyptian army marched out – and marched back again, leaving Jerusalem to its fate at the hands of Nebuchadnezzar (Jer. 37:5–10).

There is a pathetic desperation in the repetition of the words *looking* and *watched*. The Hebrew emphasizes by doubling, which the ESV captures:

> Our eyes failed, ever watching
> vainly for help;
> in our watching we watched
> for a nation which could not save.

Could not, or would not? Either or both, for whichever it was, they *did not* save. There was only one source of salvation for Israel, and it wasn't Egypt (or any other nation). And since they had turned their one and only saving God into their enemy by their incorrigible centuries of rebellion, God would not save them either.[25] At least, not from the present, immediate reality of judgment. Two generations would pass before the language of God's salvation would resound again in their ears and voices.

b. No escape (4:18–19)

These verses probably portray the final rush of the Babylonian soldiers through the streets and squares of Jerusalem, once the wall was breached,

---

[25] 'No nation could save them when the attackers are agents of God' (O'Connor, p. 67).

pursuing and slaughtering all they could find. The second line of verse 18 expresses with breathless brevity the sense of final doom in those streets:

Our end was near, our days were numbered,
*   for our end had come.*

Some of the people of Jerusalem managed to escape in the confusion, out into the wild countryside. King Zedekiah, his court and his soldiers did so by night. But, as verse 19 succinctly puts it, even in the mountains and wilderness the Babylonians were *swifter than eagles*, swooping on their prey. Hardly surprising, when the hunters were rampantly victorious soldiers and the hunted were diseased and weakened by eighteen months of siege that had ended in gruesome famine. Judah was infested by Babylon. There was simply nowhere to go.

c. No hope (4:20)

The final humiliation. They had trusted in their city. It was captured, and within weeks would be a heap of smouldering ruins. They had trusted in the temple of the Lord. It had been 'raped' by gloating pagan soldiers, and it too would be razed and burnt. And they had trusted in their king. For was he not indeed *the Lord's anointed*? And did not Psalm 2 promise that the Lord's anointed would be established securely in Zion and rule over the nations with an iron sceptre? Surely, then, God would protect his own anointed one and empower him to lead them to victory even out of the jaws of defeat.

It was not to be.

Since verse 20 almost certainly has Zedekiah in mind, we know exactly what happened to him.

The Babylonian army pursued them and overtook Zedekiah in the plains of Jericho. They captured him and took him to Nebuchadnezzar king of Babylon at Riblah in the land of Hamath, where he pronounced sentence on him. There at Riblah the king of Babylon slaughtered the sons of Zedekiah before his eyes and also killed all the nobles of Judah. Then he put out Zedekiah's eyes and bound him with bronze shackles to take him to Babylon.
(Jer. 39:5–7; 2 Kgs 25:5–7)

Such was the tragic fate of *our very life breath* (lit. 'the breath of our nostrils'), the one 'of whom we said, "Under his shadow we shall live among the nations"' (ESV).[26] But now, with the king captured and as good as dead, what hope could there be of any future life for the nation? No longer would they **live** *among the nations*; rather, they would die the death of exile among the nations. Verse 20 seems to snuff out all hope. What future could there possibly be for a people without their city, their temple, their king, and (as it must have seemed) without their God?

> Lamentations has already described the loss of much of the populace, of the impregnable Holy City, and of the very House of YHWH. It now seems to put the nail in the coffin by speaking of a rupture in the Davidic dynasty. Such a thing had never happened in the centuries-long history of the royal line! Is this the end?[27]

And yet, and yet . . .

Does the sequence of being hunted, trapped in a pit and facing an inescapable end (18–20) jog our memories? That was precisely the experience recounted by the Man in 3:52–54. But in his testimony, he had cried out to God from the pit and God had rescued him. Now that Israel has reached exactly the same point of utter paralysis, with no hope of salvation from any other nation (17), and no hope from their king, *caught in their traps* (20) – where else could they turn but to the Lord? And if they would do so, might not the testimony of the Man in chapter 3 become their testimony too, eventually if not immediately? That is what leads us to chapter 5, which is a last desperate prayer from the pit, by the whole community.

But before that, one more surprise reversal awaits us.

4. 'Comfort, comfort my people' (4:21–22)

Rejoice and be glad! That's the first surprise. Could there be any human being capable of rejoicing in the midst of the horrors described in this whole chapter? The words shock us, until we see to whom they are

---

[26] This verse is often used as an argument against the likelihood of Jeremiah being the author of Lamentations. But that may not be as convincing as it sounds. See the discussion in the Introduction, section 1b, pp. 5–9.

[27] Parry, p. 142. To feel the full flavour of the shock of the loss of the Davidic king – in apparent contradiction to God's immense and trusted promises – read the whole of Ps. 89. Note especially the sharp disjunction between vv. 37 and 38.

addressed – Lady Edom. And then we perceive their sharp irony. From the prophet Obadiah and others we know that Edom not only refused to help Judah when Nebuchadnezzar invaded, but rejoiced in the downfall of Jerusalem, took advantage of it to seize some of Judah's wealth, and assisted in the capture of the fleeing population (Obad. 11–14). 'Go ahead then,' says the Poet. 'Enjoy your treachery while you can, but know that God's judgment is coming your way soon.' *The cup* was a standard metaphor for the wrath of God – metaphorically filled with a wine that would lead to drunkenness and exposure (21b, 22b).[28] Edom will be judged and punished as Judah had been; such is the grim affirmation that effectively answers Lady Zion's appeal in 1:21–22 and the Man's in 3:60–66.

And then, out of the blue, a single line of assurance to Lady Zion herself. While Edom's judgment is yet to come, Judah's is 'completed'.

Tām is the first Hebrew word of the last verse of this final acrostic poem in Lamentations (22). 'It is finished' would translate it well. Something has been accomplished, completed, ended. The NIV takes it as a 'precative perfect' – that is, expressing a future event as though already having happened: *Your punishment will end.* However, once again we have the ambiguity that the subject of the verb is simply *'ăwōnēk*, which can mean either 'your wickedness' or 'the punishment of your wickedness'. The implication seems to be that God is declaring that the destruction of Jerusalem and all that went with it for the people, city, temple and king constitutes the *complete* outpouring of his wrath on the sin of his people. Hence the NRSV and ESV seem preferable: 'The punishment of your iniquity, O daughter Zion, is accomplished.' The judgment has been delivered, the punishment fully carried out (cf. v. 11). It is over. It is finished.

Well, not quite. The exile had just begun. But that would not last for ever. The second line of the verse assures them, *he will not prolong your exile,*[29] implying that it too will come to an end eventually. And that bald statement is filled out by the words of several prophets who looked forward to a homecoming and a rebuilding – a great reversal in which the enemies of God and Israel would be desolate, while God's presence in Zion would be re-established for ever.[30] The great announcement of Isaiah

---

[28] E.g. Pss 60:3; 75:8; Isa. 51:17; Jer. 25:15–17; Ezek. 23:32–34. Cf. Matt. 20:22–23; 26:39.

[29] Which, conversely, seems a better translation by the NIV than the NRSV/ESV, 'he will keep you in exile no longer' – which was hardly true at that point, when the exile was just beginning and would last two generations.

[30] Note especially the parallels between these closing verses of Lam. 4 and Joel 3:17–21.

40:1–2 lies ahead. As Adele Berlin says, 'This is the most hopeful note in the entire book of Lamentations.'[31]

Hopeful, certainly, but oh how slender! A single penultimate line out of the forty-four lines in the chapter. But as always in the Bible, the power of hope lies not in the quantity of rhetoric that expresses it, but in the character of the One in whom that hope is placed. That is why the voices who speak the very next line (5:1) address God directly, and continue to do so to the end of the book.

Reflections

1. In what ways do the failures of leaders in today's church, in your own context and around the world, bring disgrace and judgment on the church itself? In the light of that, what kind of leaders should we pray for and train?
2. Have there been situations where your 'eyes failed, looking in vain for help', but you found there was no help and no escape? What happened then?

---

[31] Berlin, p. 114.

Lamentations 5:1–22

5. Restore us to yourself

Prayer fills the last chapter of the book, but not because prayer is the last resort. Already Lady Zion has raised her voice in abject appeal to God, pleading with him to pay attention to her suffering. 'Look, LORD . . .' she has cried repeatedly (1:9c, 11c, 20a; 2:20–22). Those have been short outbursts, however, marked by desperation and exhaustion. Now the Poet leads the people in a sustained act of prayer. He picks up Lady Zion's longing for God just to 'look, and see', but fills it out in several ways.

First of all, he sets out the realities of the dire situation in which the people now exist. There is a struggle just to survive in the face of constant harassment from the occupying forces of the conqueror (2–10). There is the shame of cruel and degrading treatment at the hands of those enemies (11–14). There is deep and darkening sorrow over the destruction of Jerusalem and its temple (15–18). Then, second (and as his concluding effort to bring comfort to the comfortless), he recalls both the prophetic word of hope that had ended chapter 4 (4:22a) and his earlier glimpses of the abiding faithfulness and mercy of God (3:22–24), and turns them both into a final appeal to Israel's sovereign God not to abandon them for ever.

The situation described in verses 2–18 would seem to be most likely located among the surviving people in the land of Judah after the destruction of Jerusalem. The book of Jeremiah gives us a graphic picture of the miserable months before some of them, against Jeremiah's advice, took the road to refuge in Egypt (Jer. 39 – 43). The language of Lamentations 5 seems to speak eloquently for their suffering, homeless and harried as they were and wracked by continuing conflict and bloodshed from within and without.

Remember, LORD . . . look, and see (1). The words have powerful resonance beyond their obvious repetition of the previous appeals for God to
pay attention to his people's suffering. For these are exodus words. When
God remembers, it is not because God has forgotten. Rather, it means
that God will now take action on the matter he chooses to remember. So,
when the Israelites 'groaned' and 'cried out' in Egypt, 'their cry for help
because of their slavery went up to God. God heard their groaning and he
remembered his covenant with Abraham, with Isaac and with Jacob.
So God looked on the Israelites and was concerned about them' (Exod.
2:23–25). Could not the God of the exodus do the same now? Even if they
know that their suffering is suffused with God's judgment on their sin,
would God not in mercy 'look and see', 'remember' and act? That much
at least could be hoped for, when you know the God of the story you
are in. If the story had an exodus in its past, could it not also have an exodus
in its future?

1. Struggling to survive (5:1–10)

What then should God *look* at *and see*? Basically, *our disgrace* (1) – a
disgrace with several components, all of them deeply shaming. They had
felt secure, comfortably wrapped in what they thought was an indestructible fabric woven together by the strong threads of kinship, land and
covenant relationship with YHWH. Now those threads had been ripped
apart and they creep around, exposed and vulnerable, in fragile hunger
games of survival.

The terms in verse 2 are deeply rooted in pre-exilic Israel's social and
economic reality. The land as a whole was spoken of as Israel's *inheritance.*
Although it was still owned by YHWH as the supreme landlord,[1] it had been
gifted to Israel as YHWH's firstborn son, their inheritance from him. Their
life in the land was therefore a monumental tangible proof of their covenantal relationship with YHWH. They were God's people in God's land.[2] So,
if you were an Israelite living on the land before the exile, the combination
of having a place within Israel's kinship system (your belonging to a

---

[1] 'The land is mine' (Lev. 25:23).

[2] Hence the title of my book which explores the theological and ethical dimensions of Israel's economic
system, including detailed discussions of the links between kinship, land and covenant membership:
Christopher J. H. Wright, *God's People in God's Land: Family, Land and Property in the Old Testament* (Grand
Rapids: Eerdmans; Carlisle: Paternoster, 1990).

'father's house', within a clan, within one of the tribes of Israel), along with enjoying your family's 'portion' in the land that was the nation's 'inheritance' (the same Hebrew term was used for both), was an essential proof and benefit of belonging securely within the covenant people of YHWH. Conversely, those who were *strangers* and *foreigners* had no firm standing within the covenant community (though there were conditions on which they could participate in its rites), precisely because they lacked this twin criterion of kinship and land within Israel. For this reason, the foreigner (who had no land) and the eunuch (who could produce no family) rightly believed they were excluded from YHWH's people – until YHWH himself made them a promise that transcended both (Isa. 56:1–8).

But now . . . !

Another terrible reversal has happened (as if ch. 4 had not turned things upside down often enough). *Our inheritance* (the land itself) and *our homes* (the word includes not just buildings but whole households) are now occupied and dominated by the very *strangers* and *foreigners* who would once have had no share in them at all. The despised outsiders have become the lords and masters of the realm. The shame and disgrace, and the theological shock, would have been deep and unbearable. The firstborn son (Exod. 4:22) and heir is a stranger in his own house. The people of God are foreigners in God's own land.

More shock follows (3). *Strangers* and *foreigners* describe those who had previously had no share in the land (but who now, in the form of Babylonian occupying forces, are in control of it – v. 2). *Widows* and orphans were those who had no *family*. They lacked the natural protection and security of the strong kinship network that was an integral part of the covenant relationship in social and personal experience. But now the Israelites themselves, once secure in their landed households (the Heb. term for these extended families is 'father's house'), have been reduced to the level of such marginal, vulnerable people. The Hebrew word order is emphatic: 'Orphans we have become with no father; our mothers like widows.' Adele Berlin speaks of the 'outrageousness of the loss . . . the most basic element of the social structure – the family unit and the mechanism for preserving its continuity through inheritance – have been wiped out. Verses 2 and 3 are saying that there are no patrimonies and no fathers.'[3] And in speaking thus, they describe as an experienced reality

---

[3] Berlin, pp. 117–118.

what Deuteronomy had originally portrayed as one of the curses that would fall on Israel for persistent disobedience to their covenant Lord – the shattering break-up of the social and economic life of Israel's families (Deut. 28:30–33).

But there is another stark irony here. Among the many ways in which Israel had ignored the covenant laws of God was their chronic neglect of precisely those categories of people whom God commanded them to care for – widows, orphans and foreigners. The constant demand is there in the Law, the Prophets and the wisdom literature, while God's personal concern for such people is celebrated in the Psalms.[4] But for generations, far from championing the rights of the family-less and landless, they had trampled on them. And the destruction of Jerusalem was, in part, the judgment of God for that collective social sin. Now, having failed to care for the oppressed, they have joined the ranks of the oppressed themselves. Thus does the judgment of God make evil done bounce back on evildoers.

> Has not God urged repeatedly through the prophets, mercy toward 'widows and orphans and strangers at the gate'?
>
> This is plain, brute fact. What we once beheld, mercifully or otherwise – that we have become. We are the 'strangers . . . foreigners . . . orphans . . . fatherless . . . widowed . . .'
>
> Bonds that once held close in blood or friendship are sundered.
>
> Behold the once powerful, the citizens of empire; we are the outsiders, the vulnerable. We must stretch out our hands to others (above all, to Another!).[5]

So what does it mean to be treated as foreigners in your own land under occupation? To be 'internally displaced' in the land you have lived on for generations and centuries? There are peoples in the world today who could answer (like Lam. 5) with depressing details of the struggle for water supplies and heating fuel, of inflated prices for basic foods, of the constant harassment of army checkpoints, of dangerous and difficult travel, and suffocating military presence. That is what Judah experienced under

---

[4] As a tiny selection of such texts, see e.g. Exod. 23:9; Lev. 19:33–34; Deut. 14:28–29; 24:19–22; Ps. 146:7–9; Prov. 14:31; 19:17; 31:8–9; Job 29:12–17; Isa. 1:23; 10:1–2; Jer. 22:1–5.

[5] Berrigan, p. 114.

Babylonian occupation in the immediate aftermath of the fall of Jerusalem. They have to pay for the basic commodities of their own land that
they used to own (4). They are constantly being pushed to exhaustion by
soldiers (5).[6] They suffer the humiliation of doing deals with former
enemies in order to get basic food supplies (6).[7] They, who had once been
a nation of slaves, freed by the mighty power of God (in the exodus), are
now ruled over by the lowest ranks of the conquering enemy (*Slaves rule
over us*), with no hope of an exodus in sight (8). Even food grown in
attempted secrecy in the wilderness (the possible meaning of v. 9) is
a dangerous business with the seeming omnipresence of the enemy. A
people whose national narrative began with water, manna and quails in
the wilderness now find nothing but a *sword in the desert*. Disease and
hunger stalked the land even after the siege was over (10).

But in the midst of all this trauma and turmoil, they confess the reason
why (7). They have cried out and protested to God at the extremity of
suffering caused by the siege and the final orgy of slaughter and destruction. But they know the roots of it all lie in their own rebellion, and they
know that their rebellious history stretches back generations. Israel's
memory held plenty of God's good things, but engulfed by the day of
God's anger and its aftermath, now it holds only guilt. 'It is night and
memory bleeds. The ghost named guilt, fantastic, larger than life, walks
the cave of the mind.'[8]

It would be wrong to interpret verse 7 as a self-excusing statement. That
is, we should not read into it the same spirit that lies behind the proverb
quoted by both Jeremiah and Ezekiel, in which some of the exiles at least
seemed to blame previous generations for all the evils that had incurred
God's judgment, while exonerating themselves from any blame.[9] Could
such a self-righteous sentiment find a place in the agony of this prayer
with its appeal to God from a people who know their own sin (16b) and

---

[6] *At our heels* translates a Hebrew idiom, 'upon our necks', which may mean something like 'breathing
down our necks', or possibly actual yoking together of captives. 'We are shackled and yoked, driven like
beasts, weary, and have no rest' (Slavitt, *Lamentations*, p. 83).

[7] *We submitted to . . .* translates the Heb. 'we gave a hand to', which may mean 'made a pact with' (NRSV).
Assyria, if taken literally, would be an anachronism since that empire had long gone. Probably it is a general
reference to Mesopotamia, and here could mean the Babylonians – the very enemy they were subject to.
Egypt is ironic, of course, since they had hoped for military salvation from that quarter, and now are reduced
to begging bread from them.

[8] Berrigan, pp. 120–121.

[9] Jer. 31:29–30; Ezek. 18:1–4 (to which the rest of that chapter is an answer). I thus disagree with Kathleen
O'Connor's statement that the speakers in ch. 5 'interrupt the catalogue of terrors only briefly to blame their
ancestors for their suffering (5:7)' (pp. 73–74).

need of repentance and restoration (21)? On the contrary, the Poet has articulated an unquestionably sincere awareness that the sin of his people includes the *present* generation as well as the accumulated sins of *previous* generations. Read through the painful references to sin and explicit confession in every chapter – 1:5, 8, 14, 18, 20, 22; 2:14; 3:40–42; 4:6, 13; 5:16. So, yes, the present generation is indeed bearing the full weight of punishment for the sins of many generations, but *not* as innocent victims of someone else's sin. When the axe of God's judgment fell, it had to fall at some particular moment. That may seem, from one point of view, unfair. But seen from another perspective – most especially in view of the warning after warning from prophet after prophet – it is a remarkable testament to the patience and grace of God that the axe had not fallen long before.

2. Suffering in shame (5:11–14)

The focus shifts from the *economic* humiliations endured by the population at large to the *social* shame being inflicted on some particular groups in the community.

The humiliation of the enemy by the systematic rape of women,[10] married and unmarried (11), is one of the most evil dimensions of war in every age, including today. Undoubtedly it was not merely a horrendously magnified sexual offence, but also, as Kathleen O'Connor points out, 'a weapon of insult and destruction against the entire people . . . a tactic of humiliation and subjugation of the men who should protect [the women]. It attacked the nation's "purity" . . . and it attempted to eradicate the bloodlines of the people.'[11]

Violent contempt for women is matched by lack of respect for social rank or age (12). Those who had held seats of highest honour in every community, the *elders*, find that 'their faces' (Heb.) are given no dignity at all. But worse, *princes* have been subject to torture or execution or both. It is not clear exactly what being *hung up by their hands* meant (was it a form of torture, or impalement on poles with hands extended, or some

---

[10] The verb translated *violated* or 'raped' in v. 11 has strong overtones of being humiliated by deliberately inflicted violence.

[11] O'Connor, p. 76. But it is hardly true to add, as she does, 'The rape of women had little importance as an offence against the women themselves . . . The particular pain of women finds no expression in this verse.' Surely it does! The suffering of women has been highlighted throughout the book (1:4c, 18c; 2:10c, 12, 20b, 21b; 3:51; 4:10), and even personified in Lady Zion herself.

pre-Roman form of crucifixion, or bodies being hung up on display after execution?). But whatever it involved, it very graphically mixed public shame with physical agony and probably death. And that for the highest in the land.

The rest of the population did not escape the general subjugation that conquerors impose on populations. Grinding grain was a domestic chore usually done by women or slaves. Now even strapping young men[12] are tethered to the humiliating task, while younger Israelite boys collapse under the weight of wood that would once have been carried by those whom Israel had used since the days of Joshua as 'hewers of wood and drawers of water' (13; Josh. 9:27, kjv). This latter conquest had reduced the descendants of Joshua's conquest to the level of the conquered Canaanites.

And so the social life of the community has been destroyed from top to bottom. There is no functioning leadership or governance in the public arena[13] by *the elders* (14a), and there is no joyful celebration of music among the youth. Israelite society, as it had been known for centuries, has effectively come to a dead end. Apart from the sobs of the raped, the groans of the hanged and the gasping of the overloaded, nothing but the silence of a whole culture trampled underfoot.

3. Sorrowing for Zion (5:15–18)

And so lament can be the only form of song left to the people, as the Poet leads them onwards to the climax of their prayer. *Joy* and *dancing* have been left behind (15), and it will still be an unanswered question by the end of the chapter whether they will ever return. For the present, there is nothing but the shame of the conquered and the remorse of the sinner (16). *The crown has fallen from our head* may have a literal meaning in the capture of King Zedekiah, but it could metaphorically mean the loss of all that had given dignity, honour and national sovereignty to their tiny but ancient nation and its renowned capital city.

Woe to us is a mournful self-accusing echo of every 'Woe!' that generations of prophets had uttered in condemnation and warning since Amos of Tekoa some hundred and fifty years earlier. The four Hebrew words of

---

[12] The Hebrew word is used of men in their prime, particularly soldiers.

[13] *The city gate* was the place where all public business was conducted – business deals, court cases, political decisions, etc. Cf. Ruth 4:1–2; Job 29:7; Prov. 31:23, 31.

verse 16b ('Woe-indeed to-us for we-have-sinned') may be the shortest, simplest and deepest moment of self-awareness in the book.[14] Indeed, they are perhaps the most concise condensing of the essence of repentance in Scripture, echoed by the tax collector in Jesus' parable: 'The tax collector . . . would not even look up to heaven, but beat his breast and said, "God, have mercy on me, a sinner"' (Luke 18:13). On the foundation of this clear-eyed but tear-filled acknowledgment, the Poet will lead the people to appeal to God for the grace of repentance and restoration (21). We may hope, though the book gives no answer from God, that their prayer will meet the same ultimate assurance that Jesus promised the penitent tax collector – 'those who humble themselves will be exalted'.

But as yet any such assurance and exaltation are a far distant dream. *This . . . these things* (17) points to an excruciating and unrelieved present reality. The emphatic words point back to all the horrors that have been described in the prayer so far, and they point forward to the summation of it all: *Mount Zion . . . lies desolate* (18). For *that* 'our hearts are sick. Our eyes are dim with tears.'[15] No more personification of Zion as a lady, showing yet shielding the sheer facts in metaphor. Recalling 2:5–9, the actual earthy reality is spoken: *Mount Zion*, once a holy city set on a hill, is now a mound of charred rubble defiled by unclean scavenging *jackals*. Behold Zion, 'the city of our God, his holy mountain', about which 'glorious things' can no longer now be spoken (Pss 48:1–3; 87:3). Behold 'the mountain of the LORD's temple', not raised as a beacon to which all nations would stream (Isa. 2:2), but razed to the ground, trampled by the nations, soaked in blood, ravaged by pestilence, sword and fire, reduced to dust and death. Behold 'the joy of the whole earth' become the world's laughing stock. What now of the joyful anticipation of those who thrilled to the invitation, 'Let us go to the house of the LORD' (Ps. 122:1)? What now of the confident faith of those who sang that 'those who trust in the LORD are like Mount Zion, which cannot be shaken but endures for ever' (Ps. 125:1)?

One verse, only seven Hebrew words – but Lamentations 5:18 sums up the catastrophe of this whole book that has tolled the death knell of Israel's land, Israel's city, Israel's king, Israel's temple, Israel's faith, Israel itself as the covenant people of YHWH. All collapsed, all ended. To all observers, all gone.

---

[14] Shorter even than the six words of 1:18a.

[15] Slavitt, *Lamentations*, p. 85.

And Israel's God?

Ah no! For this is *prayer.* And to whom is the prayer that began in verse 1 being addressed? '*You,* Lord' (19)!

> This opaque God, this Flail and Reaper, Judge and Prosecutor, nonetheless must be acknowledged. Faith demands it, faith pronounces it. Brought low, counting for little or nothing on the scales of this world . . . the exiles touch the heart of faith.[16]

4. Searching for God (5:19–22)

You, YHWH . . . The words are emphatic, implying without the word itself a massive Pauline '*But* . . .' In the face of all that verse 18 condenses of physical, national, emotional and theological pain, the people turn to the One they know, the named covenant God of all their history, the One who is still there precisely because they know that all this desolation is the work of his hands. The prayer reaches its climax in an astounding leap of faith across the chasm of defeat, destruction and death. The prayer reaches out from the ruins of God's dwelling-place on earth and touches the eternal throne of God in heaven.

For that indeed is the breathtaking paradox and challenge of verse 19. It is, at one level, a defiant, subversive taunt of the Babylonian conqueror. Who did they think they had defeated? Rebellious Jerusalem, of course. And why had they pillaged, destroyed and burnt Jerusalem's temple? To demonstrate the victory of the gods of Babylon over just another god, as they thought, the god of Israel – according to their understanding of the ways of heaven and earth. But if that was what they thought, or if that was what any shattered Israelites were tempted to think, they could not be more wrong. Yes, the temple of YHWH lay in ruins. But who had done it? Well, Nebuchadnezzar, of course. But as Jeremiah and Lamentations make so uncomfortably clear, behind the hammer of Nebuchadnezzar was the hand of YHWH.

Israel's God had destroyed his own temple?! Unthinkable to the Babylonians. Unthinkable to most Israelites who had never listened to Jeremiah. But no longer unthinkable to those being led in prayer by the Poet of Lamentations.

---

16 Berrigan, p. 128.

But at another level, of course, that bad news (that YHWH in his sovereignty had destroyed his own temple through the agency of a nation doing his bidding) was ultimately good news, and the only foundation for hope. YHWH himself remained on the *throne*! 'The temple may be destroyed but God's throne is indestructible.'[17] The sovereign governance of YHWH, God of heaven and earth, was not threatened in the least by the destruction of a building which, as Israel had acknowledged since its foundation, could not in any case contain him. 'Will God really dwell on earth?' Solomon had asked in his prayer of dedication. 'The heavens, even the highest heaven, cannot contain you. How much less this temple I have built!' (1 Kgs 8:27). YHWH was not dependent on the temple. Not only did he not need it in the first place, but he could and would destroy it (as Jeremiah predicted at the risk of his own life, and as Jesus did too, of course, at the cost of his), when it became the irredeemable hotbed of covenant-breaking idolatry and social evils (Jer. 7 and 26). And thus indeed it had happened.

But from the desolation of the temple (18), they could still affirm the transcendent truth of Israel's creed – sung from ancient days but never more needed than now:

You, LORD, reign for ever;
   your throne endures from generation to generation.
(19)

The juxtaposition of verses 18 and 19 is powerful – poetically and theologically. From the lowest point of Israel's degradation – the desolation and defilement of Mount Zion (God's address on earth, as it were) – we are catapulted to the highest place in (or rather beyond) the universe – the enduring throne of God.

God's glory had left the earthly building even before it was destroyed.[18] But God himself had not been toppled from his heavenly throne. Let the penitent Israelites remember to whom they were praying.

The creator of heaven and earth governs all that takes place within them. His temple is the whole cosmos. His reign transcends any physical building, though it has an impact on every earthly reality and every historical chain of events.

---

[17] Berlin, p. 125.

[18] As Ezekiel saw in his vision of the evils in the temple and the glory of God departing (Ezek. 8 – 10) – a vision he had among the first group of exiles before the final fall of the city.

'Heaven is my throne,
    and the earth is my footstool.
Where is the house you will build for me?
    Where will my resting-place be?
Has not my hand made all these things,
    and so they came into being?'
            declares the LORD.
(Isa. 66:1–2)

The words of verse 19 are echoed in a psalm which possibly (though not necessarily) comes from the same terrible moment as Lamentations. Psalm 102 has as its heading, 'A prayer of an afflicted person who has grown weak and pours out a lament before the LORD' – a description that sounds uncannily similar to the major voice of Lamentations. And at the heart of the psalm lies the affirmation,

But you, LORD, sit enthroned for ever;
    your renown endures through all generations.

If such an echo is found here, then the following verses of the psalm would generate hope. They go on to invite God to 'arise and have compassion on Zion'. They look forward to the day when 'the LORD will rebuild Zion', so that future generations will have cause to 'praise the LORD' (Ps. 102:12–18).

Verse 19, then, radically shifts the perspective of the whole prayer, and the whole book. It provides a foundation for hope, but cannot yet summon hope's certainty. God is still on the throne, but will he remember his own? That is the question, and remains a question for the present.

For indeed, the present seems still like an interminably extended endurance of God's forgetting (20). And at such a time the cry of so many biblical laments is precisely *Why . . . ? Why . . . ?* 'Why forever do you forget us, forsake us for length of days?' Even when every admission of sin has been made, even when every acceptance of divine judgment has been spoken, the days are long. The pain seems unending. 'My God, my God, why have you forsaken me?' cried another psalmist, along with others.[19] And yet, even the form of the question – addressed to 'you', *You, LORD* – assumes some continuing relationship with YHWH as their covenant God.

---

[19] Ps. 22:1; cf. 77:7–9; 79:5; and most desperately of all, the whole of Ps. 88.

For if he had *ceased* to be the God of that covenant commitment, then why should he *not* forsake and forget them? The agony of the question lies in the pain of a *broken* relationship, not in the assumption of a relationship so irredeemably severed that it no longer exists at all.

Verse 20 is the last question in the book, and like all the other ones, it gets no answer. God does not explain. The prophets have done that already. God does not set a time limit to his judgment. Other prophets will do that too. For the Poet and the people whose prayer he is voicing, the question hangs frozen in the air, challenging the frozen present, the unbearable 'Now' of bearing the judgment of God in the day of his anger.

So when the question remains unanswered, all that is left is a final appeal (21). But how the appeal has changed! All the appeals addressed directly to YHWH so far in the book have been seeking to get his attention, to draw him down into the situation, to get him to 'look and see'. And that, we have seen, is totally understandable in the terrifying suffering of the people, Lady Zion. YHWH is the God who sees (Gen. 16:13; Exod. 2:24–25; 1 Sam. 2:3; Ps. 33:13–15), so entreating him to do so is emotionally right and theologically justified.

But here the direction of appeal changes. The people do not ask God to come down to see *them*. Rather, they ask God to cause them to return to *him*. *Restore us to yourself, LORD, that we may return.* The Hebrew is: 'Cause us to [re]turn,[20] YHWH, to you, and we shall [re]turn' (or, 'and please let us return'). Or in the classic KJV, 'Turn thou us unto thee, O LORD, and we shall be turned.' What they ask for is not that their enemies be driven away, nor that Zion be rebuilt (such things can wait). What they want is not even just an end to their suffering. What they plead for, like Job, is to know again the presence of God himself and the assurance of their covenant relationship with him.

And they freely acknowledge that any restoration of that relationship must come from God's side. Any turning back to him will be through his divine impulse and enabling. God must take the initiative in restoring his people to himself, 'causing them to return', as the Hebrew verb expresses it.[21] In acknowledging and praying this, the Poet joins the psalmists who

---

[20] The verb is the *hiphil* (causative) form of *šûb*, to turn.

[21] Kathleen O'Connor is thus not quite correct when she writes, 'They ask for a turning around of God, for a conversion of God's heart back to them. They want God to turn from abandoning and rejecting them' (p. 78). Assuredly they do, but what they in fact ask for is for God to cause *them* to turn back to him, so that his abandonment and rejection can be ended.

made the same appeal (e.g. Ps. 80:7, 19), endorses the theology of Deuteronomy 30, in which God's grace promises to *enable* a repentant people to seek him and love him with all their heart,[22] echoes the repentant words that Jeremiah put in the mouth of Ephraim (Jer. 31:18), and anticipates the promise of Ezekiel that God would indeed initiate and accomplish the restoration of his people, by God's own grace and for God's own glory (Ezek. 36:24–28).

Such resonances we hear from the rest of Scripture, but not within our text itself. Even so, we long that Lamentations had ended with that great closing appeal of verse 21, for then we could confidently read into it all the assurance and future hope that our knowledge of the biblical God, and our vantage point of knowing the rest of the Old Testament story, inevitably generates. We've read Isaiah 40 – 55! We know what God will say, eventually if not now.[23]

But that's not where Lamentations ends.

Verse 22 cannot be avoided, though it is notoriously hard to translate. The two main verbs are crystal clear. 'Rejecting, you have rejected us,[24] you have been angry against us to the very greatest extent.' That much has been said again and again in the book. It is the patent theological explanation of the horrors that had befallen the city for the sin of its people. The crucial question is how to translate the opening two words of the verse, *kî 'im*.[25] Although the commonest rendering in our English Bibles is 'Unless . . .', my own preference lies with those who translate, 'Even if . . .' or 'Even though . . .'[26] The difference is as follows.

Unless . . .

In verse 21 the people appeal to God to restore them as of old, but then verse 22 seems to put some qualification on whether or not God would do so. The translation 'unless . . .' implies that the people think God would only restore them *if* he had *not* rejected them and *if* he were *not* still angry with them. But their present reality (as described in the whole book and

---

[22] Deut. 30:6; note how the promise of v. 6 matches the demand of vv. 2 and 10.

[23] 'Why the wailing, why this talk of "forgetting . . . abandoning", except that we knew otherwise? Our stories of Exodus tell it; once, God remembered, God cherished. What history is ours! Let it be summoned . . . Shall God now turn to stone, turn a stony ear to our plight? God shall not' (Berrigan, p. 130).

[24] The repetition being the characteristic Hebrew way of emphasizing the main verb, meaning, 'You have utterly or emphatically rejected us.'

[25] The commentaries all wrestle with the issue. Suggestions include: 'For if', 'But', 'But if', 'But instead', 'Unless', 'Even though', and turning it into a question, 'Or have you . . . ?' The best recent summaries of all the exegetical options explored by different scholars are provided by Parry and House.

[26] Parry, pp. 156–157; House, pp. 470–471.

still there in ch. 5) strongly suggests that he has and he is. So the most likely implication of opening verse 22 with 'unless . . .' is to inject a negative suspicion into the prayer. The Poet writes: *Unless you have utterly rejected us and are angry with us beyond measure* – and thinks under his breath: 'which is probably the case. Our appeal has fallen on deaf ears. This is God's final and irreversible abandonment of Israel.'[27] Of course, it is possible to read the verse beginning with 'unless . . .' and still be hopeful that what it says might not remain true, and so God will answer the prayer. The ambiguity remains, but a negative result seems the most likely. Lamentations then ends in lingering uncertainty sliding towards despair. 'With thinning hope and flagging energy, the voices drift away.'[28]

Even if / even though . . .

In verse 21 the people appeal to God to restore them as of old, but then in verse 22 immediately *repeat and acknowledge* the fact of God's great anger, demonstrated in their present terrible plight. In other words, there is no question but that God has indeed *rejected* his people and is indeed exceedingly *angry* with them. The Law and the Prophets had threatened exactly such an outcome if they persisted in covenant-breaking rebellion. They were reaping what they had sown. The whole book assumes that perspective. Granted that in the course of the book there have been questions and protests about the appalling severity of their suffering. Was it not excessive, and beyond all human endurance or divine justification? That might be so; God does not answer those accusations, though there are hints, as we saw, that God himself weeps with his people at the Babylonian brutality and cruelty that had served as the fallen human instrument of his judgment. But for all that, the Poet and the people have not drawn back from acknowledging (in every chapter) the fact of their own sin and rebellion, and the fact that sin and rebellion on their part had resulted in rejection and wrath on God's part. And that is where they now languish. Verse 22 states a continuing tragic reality that they fully understand.

Nevertheless . . . in spite of their full awareness of God's rejection and anger, they know their God well enough to make the classic appeal of verse 21. Rejection and anger, however awful and exceedingly great, however endless they seem to be in the present experience of unrelieved

---

[27] Most succinctly expressed by Kathleen O'Connor's summary of vv. 21–22: 'We might entitle the people's final prayer, "What God Should Do, But Probably Will Not"' (p. 77).

[28] O'Connor, p. 79.

pain, need not be the *eternal* reality. Will they not come to an end? Is that not what their psalms affirm and their history demonstrates? Is that not precisely what the Poet himself had affirmed in 3:31–32?[29] Noticeably, 5:22 does not use the word normally translated 'for ever'. It simply doubles the verb of rejection and intensifies the verb of anger. That is where they are now – under God's utter rejection and extreme anger. But out of that acknowledged reality, and even in spite of it, they cry out to God for restoration.

Verse 22, then, is an acceptance of the divine truth about the facts of their situation, not a (probably forlorn) hope that the truth might be otherwise. The Poet leads his people to pray the appeal of verse 21 *even in the face of* the truth acknowledged in verse 22, not hoping that verse 22 might somehow not be true, while fearing that it might be and probably is.

Suppose the Poet had chosen to put verses 21 and 22 the other way round? We might then naturally have read them with the assumption that God's rejection and anger are accepted facts (especially if verse 22 had followed immediately after the poignant question of verse 20), followed by a final climactic appeal for God nevertheless to restore them. The book would then have ended with clearly implied hope. God would surely answer its closing prayer, if verse 21 had been the closing words of the book.[30]

But the Poet did *not* end his book that way, and we must respect his very deliberate placing of verse 22 at the end. What is the impact of ending the prayer and the book with words of rejection and wrath? In summary, my view is *not* that he thereby places the previous verses (including the affirmation of 19 and the appeal of 21) under a cloud of suspicion and negativity, leaving us thinking that ultimately there may be no hope at all of restoration. Rather, he places those verses (including the positive truth of 19 and the implicit hope on which the appeal of 21 is grounded) *within the context* of a continuing present suffering that must not be forgotten or minimized. Readers must not be allowed to forget whose voice we are hearing. This is the voice of those *still enduring* present suffering and seeing no end in sight yet. The affirmation and prayer (19, 21) come from the centre of a storm that has not yet abated (22). Even if, in God's mercy, the future may hold relief and restoration, the present is unbearably painful.

---

[29] A significant support for translating *kî 'im* as 'even if' in 5:22 is that the same expression clearly has that meaning in 3:32: 'Even if he causes grief, he will have compassion, according to the greatness of his mercies.'

[30] Interestingly, it is the custom among Jews, when reading Lamentations, to repeat v. 21 at the end after v. 22, presumably in order to allow that hope to surface and sustain.

The last verse of the book is thus consistent with the whole of it. This *is* our reality, says the Poet on behalf of his people. This *is* our pain. And no matter what lies ahead in the sovereignty of God, we will make sure you hear, and see, and know what we have gone through here and now. Lamentations thus ends where it began, with the awful continuing reality of the present suffering of the Poet and his people. But it does not quite end *as* it began, for on the journey it has allowed the light of what is known about God to penetrate the apparent absence and silence of God with some rays of truth.

In other words, just as the awful deathly darkness of Israel's destruction cannot extinguish the flickering light of Israel's hope (piercing the darkness in the centre of ch. 3), neither should the reminder of the faith of the psalmists (19) stifle the questioning cry from the depths of horror and suffering (20, 22). Both speak truth. Both must be heard, and neither can delegitimize the other. That is the brave but brilliant balance achieved in the closing verses of this profound poem.

It is not necessary, then, to interpret the ending of Lamentations so negatively as to assume that it dashes all hope, as some do in order to honour the genuine reality of seemingly unending suffering (of Old Testament Israel or in today's world). Two examples of that tendency among recent scholars are Adele Berlin and Kathleen O'Connor. Their concern for honesty on behalf of those who suffer (in ancient Israel or today) is admirable, but it seems they overstate their case to make the point.

Adele Berlin agrees that the affirmation of verse 19 should bring hope to the Judeans.

> But this hope is dashed immediately by God's refusal to respond . . .
> Just as God exists forever, so his abandonment of Israel goes on forever,
> or so it seems to our poet [*though, as pointed out above, he does not
> say 'for ever'*] . . . Verse 21 pleads that the former relationship between
> God and the people may be reinstated; but v. 22 ends the prayer on
> a note of despair and a feeling of permanent rejection. The last chapter,
> and the book as a whole, fail to provide the comfort that has been
> sought throughout it. The book thereby remains a perpetual lament
> commemorating unconsolable [*sic*] suffering.[31]

---

[31] Berlin, p. 125.

I would agree with that last sentence. The book does indeed stand in Scripture as a 'perpetual lament' speaking for those whose present suffering is inconsolable. As such it is probably the most powerful voice and advocate on their behalf in the whole Bible. But that does not depend on assuming that any word of faith, or prayer of hope, is therefore 'dashed' and denied. It is not contradictory, on the one hand, to believe that God can and will ultimately bring deliverance and release, and yet on the other hand, still to cry out to him in pain, protest and baffled impatience from the midst of present suffering, wondering how long rejection and anger will continue. If psalmists can do that, why is it necessary to deny that the Poet of Lamentations could do it? And plenty of believers in Israel's God, Jews and Christians, have done exactly both.

Kathleen O'Connor writes even more graphically. She accuses those who translate the final verse with 'Even though . . .', or any other way that allows what she calls 'a happy ending', of 'distorting the Hebrew text' – even though the exegetical arguments are intricate and complex in any direction. Rather, she sees verse 22 as a nightmare ending:

> The text expresses the community's doubt about God's care and about God's character. It utters the unthinkable – that God has utterly and permanently rejected them [*though, again, verse 22 does not use a word that could mean 'permanently'*], cast them off in unrelenting anger. The verse is fearsome, a nightmare of abandonment, like a child's terror that the only ones who can protect her and give her a home have rejected her forever. Such is the ending of this book, and I think it is wonderful.
>
> It is wonderful because it is truthful, because it does not force hope prematurely, because it expresses what many in worlds of trauma and destruction know to be true. Its very unsettledness enables the book to be a house for sorrow, neither denied nor overcome with sentimental wishes, theological escapism, or premature closure. Although Lamentations does not tell the whole story and does not contain all there is to say about God's relationship to the world, it does tell truth about the human experience of suffering.[32]

Again, I can affirm that final sentence, and the apt description of Lamentations as 'a house for sorrow'. Indeed, I too think the ending of the book is

---

[32] O'Connor, p. 79.

'wonderful', for its astonishing, disturbing, challenging balance of realities and truths achieved in its final four verses. And yes, it is also 'truthful'. But in order to affirm that Lamentations speaks truth about suffering, it is not necessary to claim that Lamentations denies (or radically doubts) truth about God's character and ultimate faithfulness to his covenant mercy and purposes. Nor is it necessary to dismiss such truths about God (which Lamentations itself has affirmed at the heart of the book) with pejorative phrases like 'sentimental wishes' and 'theological escapism'. There is nothing sentimental or escapist about affirming the massive majesty of the redemptive patience, faithfulness and salvation of the biblical God in confronting and defeating the ravages of evil and sin and delivering us ultimately from all the suffering they wreak on humanity and creation.

That is the story that the rest of the Bible tells. Within that story, Lamentations has its place and its voice.[33] Speaking out of the particularity of Judah and Jerusalem in 587 BC, it touches the universality of human suffering – which, whether or not it may be deserved by the sufferer (and Job tackles that challenge), ultimately traces back to the global roots of evil, sin and rebellion, human and satanic. And that story, of course, leads to and centres upon the cross and resurrection of Jesus Christ. The two are indissolubly linked together, and each has its vital necessity. We cannot contemplate the cross without knowing of the resurrection to come (for not even Jesus did that). But equally, we cannot use our knowledge of the resurrection as a 'sentimental' or 'escapist' way of denying the absolute horror of the cross and the unimaginable depth of suffering that Christ endured at every level of his divine and human being.

But in between Good Friday and Easter Day stands Holy Saturday – the literally 'dead time' when the agony of Good Friday has done its worst, but God has not yet stretched out his right hand and mighty arm in glorious resurrecting power.

That, as Robin Parry suggests,[34] is where Lamentations positions Israel in 587 BC – along with all those in Christ who share his sufferings in this world, enduring them with ultimate hope, but without present relief and

---

[33] See the further discussion of this 'whole Bible' perspective in the Introduction, section 3, pp. 24–29.

[34] Parry, pp. 191–193. '[Reading the book in the light of the cross and resurrection] *preserves the voices of the sufferers as uttered on their Holy Saturday*. Christians cannot read Lamentations with the same hopelessness felt by Lady Jerusalem because they know that Christ has been raised. The resurrection generates a hermeneutic of hope that can transform the darkness of Lamentations and infuse it with a brighter light than any found in the book itself. But, and this is important, it does *not* make the pain of Lamentations less dreadful and dark. It does not explain why the pain was as it was. It does not trivialize the suffering any more than the resurrection trivializes the cross' (p. 191; italics original).

even with a martyr's death (cf. Rev. 6:9–11). Like them, like Christ on Holy Saturday, Israel at the end of Lamentations remains in the land of exile and death. Waiting. Resurrection has not yet been heralded. Easter Day has not yet dawned.

But it will.

It will.

Reflections

1. How important do you consider it to be that the book of Lamentations makes its final poem a prayer?
2. What does the poem itself teach us about the realism and honesty that should characterize prayer?
3. The book could hardly be said to have a 'happy ending'. But do you think it has a 'hopeful ending'? And if so, for what reasons? And if not, where would you go in the Bible to bring hope into the picture?
4. How does the book as a whole help us to keep a healthy and pastorally sensitive balance between facing up to the terrible realities of evil, suffering and death in our fallen world, and holding on to the truths the Bible teaches about the eternal character of God and the ultimate victory of the reign of God, where the book (almost) ends (5:19)?

The Bible Speaks Today:
Old Testament series

The Message of Genesis 1 – 11
The dawn of creation
David Atkinson

The Message of Genesis 12 – 50
From Abraham to Joseph
Joyce G. Baldwin

The Message of Exodus
The days of our pilgrimage
Alec Motyer

The Message of Leviticus
Free to be holy
Derek Tidball

The Message of Numbers
Journey to the Promised Land
Raymond Brown

The Message of Deuteronomy
Not by bread alone
Raymond Brown

The Message of Joshua
Promise and people
David G. Firth

The Message of Judges
Grace abounding
Michael Wilcock

The Message of Ruth
The wings of refuge
David Atkinson

The Message of 1 and 2 Samuel
Personalities, potential, politics and power
Mary J. Evans

The Message of 1 and 2 Kings
God is present
John W. Olley

The Message of 1 and 2 Chronicles
One church, one faith, one Lord
Michael Wilcock

The Message of Ezra and Haggai
Building for God
Robert Fyall

The Message of Nehemiah
God's servant in a time of change
Raymond Brown

The Message of Esther
God present but unseen
David G. Firth

The Message of Job
Suffering and grace
David Atkinson

The Bible Speaks Today:
New Testament series

The Message of 1 Timothy and Titus
The life of the local church
John Stott

The Message of 2 Timothy
Guard the gospel
John Stott

The Message of Hebrews
Christ above all
Raymond Brown

The Message of James
The tests of faith
Alec Motyer

The Message of 1 Peter
The way of the cross
Edmund Clowney

The Message of 2 Peter and Jude
The promise of his coming
Dick Lucas and Chris Green

The Message of John's Letters
Living in the love of God
David Jackman

The Message of Revelation
I saw heaven opened
Michael Wilcock